United States
Department of
Agriculture

Forest Service

**Northern
Research Station**

General Technical
Report NRS-38

Urban and Community Forests of New England

Connecticut
Maine
Massachusetts
New Hampshire
Rhode Island
Vermont

David J. Nowak
Eric J. Greenfield

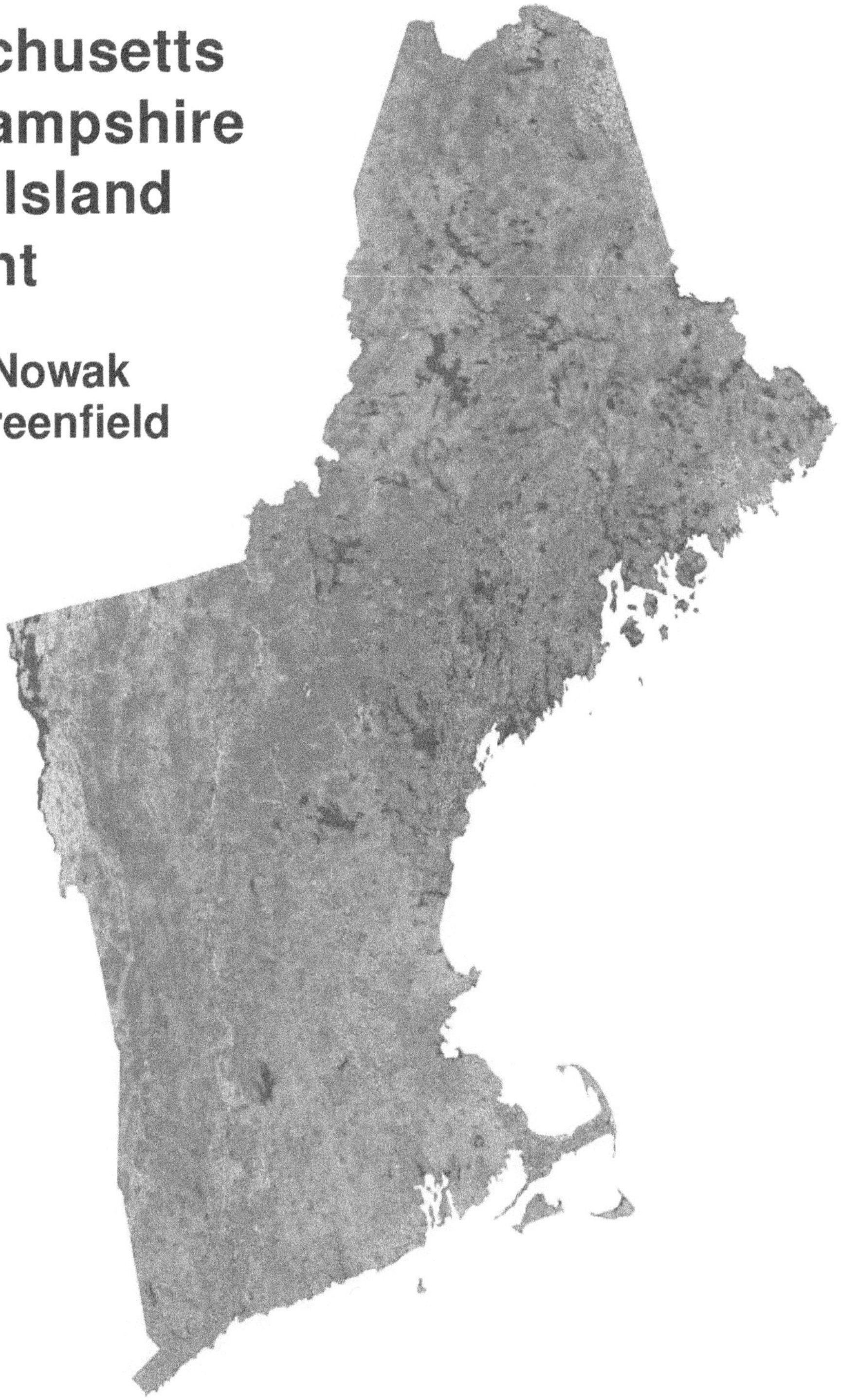

Abstract

This report details how land cover and urbanization vary within the states of Connecticut, Maine, Massachusetts, New Hampshire, Rhode Island, and Vermont by community (incorporated and census designated places), county subdivision, and county. Specifically this report provides critical urban and community forestry information for each state including human population characteristics and trends, changes in urban and community lands, tree canopy and impervious surface cover characteristics, distribution of land-cover classes, a relative comparison of urban and community forests among local government types, determination of priority areas for tree planting, and a summary of urban tree benefits. Report information can improve the understanding, management, and planning of urban and community forests. The data from this report is reported for each state on the CD provided in the back of this book, and it may be accessed by state at: http://www.nrs.fs.fed.us/data/urban.

The Authors

DAVID J. NOWAK is a research forester and project leader, and ERIC J. GREENFIELD is a research forester with the Forest Service's Northern Research Station at Syracuse, NY

CONTENTS

INTRODUCTION

As part of the Forest and Rangeland Renewable Resources Planning Act of 1974, the first national assessment of urban forests was completed in 2000 (Dwyer et al. 2000, Nowak et al. 2001b). This assessment used 1-km resolution Advanced Very-High Resolution Radiometer (AVHRR) data (Zhu 1994) and 1990 U.S. Census Bureau (2007) population and geographic data to assess urban tree cover. The assessment concluded that urban areas in the conterminous United States doubled in size between 1969 and 1994 and covered 3.5 percent of the total land area. Urban areas were estimated to contain approximately 3.8 billion trees with an average tree canopy cover of 27 percent.

To update this first report, higher resolution (30 m) tree canopy and impervious surface cover maps were used (from 2001 Landsat satellite imagery and published in 2007) (Homer et al. 2007, U.S. Geol. Surv. 2007) in conjunction with 1990 and 2000 census and geographic data (1:5,000,000 scale cartographic boundary files) (U.S. Census Bureau 2007) to assess current urban and community forest attributes. These results are being published for each of the lower 48 United States to provide information on urban change and state-specific urban and community forestry data.

This report includes information for the following states: Connecticut, Maine, Massachusetts, New Hampshire, Rhode Island, and Vermont.

Data are reported for the state, county, county subdivision, and community jurisdictions. The jurisdictional units used in this report are derived from U.S. Census (2007) geographic data and defined legal or statistical divisions. "County"[1] refers to the primary subdivision within states. "County subdivisions" are primary divisions of a county and are statistically equivalent entities for the reporting of census data. They include census county divisions (CCD), census sub areas, minor civil divisions (MCD), and unorganized territories. "Communities" are incorporated and census designated places, and consolidated cities, (U.S. Census Bureau 2007). For detailed definitions, see http://www.census.gov/geo/www/cob/cs_metadata.html (2007).

---

[1] The primary legal divisions of most states are termed "counties." In Louisiana, these divisions are known as "parishes." In four states (Maryland, Missouri, Nevada, and Virginia), there are one or more incorporated places that are independent of any county organization and thus constitute primary divisions of their states; these incorporated places are known as "independent cities" and are treated as equivalent to counties for statistical purposes. (For some statistical purposes they may be treated as county subdivisions and places.) The District of Columbia has no primary divisions, and the entire area is considered equivalent to a county for statistical purposes. (http://www.census.gov/geo/www/cob/co_metadata.html, 2007)

REPORT OVERVIEW

The information in this report can aid local and regional managers and planners of urban and community forest resources. This report provides urban and community forest reference information and data from the state to local level on the following attributes related to the urban and community forest resource:

- Human population characteristics and trends
- Urban and community land
- Tree canopy cover characteristics
- Impervious surface cover characteristics
- Classified land-cover characteristics
- Relative comparisons of urban and community forests
- Priority areas for tree planting
- Urban tree benefits

Information in this report can be used by urban and community forestry professionals to:

- Understand general land-cover characteristics and urbanization trends at several geographic scales
- Compare tree canopy cover among similar communities
- Determine areas of greatest growth and areas of highest tree planting priority
- Relate urban and community forests to pollution removal and carbon storage
- Promote more detailed and/or locally appropriate urban and community forest inventories, censuses, or field surveys (e.g., i-Tree – www.itreetools.org)
- Establish local to statewide standards related to urban and community forestry
- Support urban and community forestry programs
- Improve urban and community forest management and planning.

The remainder of this section details how information was derived for each attribute reported for the urban and community areas. The subsequent state summaries detail the findings for each state in this region. Most tables for each state are not given in this report, rather they can be found on the CD provided with this report or accessed at: http://www.nrs.fs.fed.us/data/urban.

URBAN FOREST ATTRIBUTES
Human Population Characteristics and Trends

Human population and population density changes over time, and geographic distribution are important measurements of the urban environment because human populations are an integral part of community and urban forest dynamics. Within divisions of state, county, county subdivision, and community, total population, population changes from 1990 to 2000 and population density are detailed based on U.S. Census data (U.S. Census Bureau 2007).

Urban and Community Land

Two geographic definitions overlap: "community" and "urban". The definition of community is based on jurisdictional or political boundaries delimited by U.S. Census definitions of places (U.S. Census Bureau 2007). Community lands are places of established human settlement that may include all, some, or no urban land within their boundaries.

The definition of urban is based on population density as delimited using the U.S. Census Bureau's (2007) definition: all territory, population, and housing units located within urbanized areas or urban clusters. Urbanized area and urban cluster boundaries encompass densely settled territories, which are described by one of the following:

- One or more block groups or census blocks with a population density of at least 386.1 people/ km^2 (1,000 people/mile^2)
- Surrounding block groups and census blocks with a population density of 193.1 people/ km^2 (500 people/mile^2)
- Less densely settled blocks that form enclaves or indentations, or are used to connect discontinuous areas

More specifically, urbanized areas consist of territory with 50,000 or more people. Urban clusters, a concept new to the 2000 Census, consist of territory with at least 2,500 people but fewer than 50,000 people. This new definition tends to be more restrictive than the 1990 U.S. Census urban definition and encompasses many areas typically considered suburban. The 2000 Census definition of urban was applied to 1990 Census geographic data to analyze change in urban land between 1990 and 2000 (Nowak et al. 2005).

As urban land reveals the more heavily populated areas (population density-based definition) and community land indicates both urban and rural (i.e., non-urban) communities that are recognized by their geopolitical boundaries (political definition), both definitions provide information related to human settlements and the forest resources within those settlements. As some urban land exists beyond community boundaries and not all community land is urban (i.e., communities are often a mix of urban and rural land), the category of "urban or community" was created to understand forest attributes accumulated by the union of these two definitions. The "urban or community" term used throughout this report encompasses both urban land and land in communities.

Percent urban land is a ratio of urban land over total land within a census geographic division, and percent community land is a ratio of community land over total land within the geopolitical unit. In addition, changes in urban land and changes in community land are reported between 1990 and 2000.

For each state, Tables 1 through 4 summarize the population, and urban and community land attributes for the state, communities, county subdivisions, and counties respectively (CD and http://www.nrs.fs.fed.us/data/urban).

Tree Canopy Cover Characteristics

Tree canopy cover is a critical measure of the urban and community forest resource. Tree canopy cover gives a broad indication of the overall forest resource and its associated benefits. To assess urban and community land cover characteristics, the multi-resolution land

characteristics consortium's National Land Cover Database (NLCD) was used (Homer et al. 2004, U.S. Geol. Surv. 2007, Yang et al. 2003). The NLCD, released in early 2007, was processed from 2001 Landsat satellite imagery and provides estimates of percentage tree canopy and impervious surface cover within 30-m pixels or cells across the state. The tree canopy percentages in this report are calculated using the land area (not including water) of the geopolitical units derived from the U.S. Census cartographic boundary data and NLCD. In addition to percentage tree cover, four other canopy cover attributes, derived from the same data, were assessed:

- Tree canopy cover per capita—Tree canopy cover (m^2) divided by the number of people within the area of analysis.
- Total green space—Total area minus impervious and water cover (ha). This attribute estimates pervious cover (i.e., grass, soil, or tree-covered areas).
- Canopy green space—Tree cover divided by total green space (percent). This value is the proportion of the total green space that is filled by tree canopies.
- Available green space—Total green space minus tree canopy cover (ha). This value is the amount of grass and soil area not covered with tree canopies and potentially available for planting.

Impervious Surface Cover Characteristics

Similar to tree cover, impervious surface cover provides another piece of valuable information related to the urban environment. Impervious surface cover gives an indication of an area's developed hardscape, which has important influences on urban air temperatures and water flows and also yields information on limitations to urban tree cover. Impervious surface cover also was derived from the NLCD database (U.S. Geol. Surv. 2007). The impervious surface cover percentages in this report are calculated using the land area (not including water) of the geopolitical units derived from the U.S. Census cartographic boundary data and NLCD. Impervious surface per capita is calculated from NLCD 2001 and U.S. Census data.

For each state, Tables 1, and 5 through 7 summarize the tree canopy and impervious surface cover attributes for the state, communities, county subdivisions, and counties respectively (CD and http://www.nrs.fs.fed.us/data/urban).

Classified Land-cover Characteristics

Land-cover types also are summarized using 2001 Landsat satellite data that were classified with the U.S. Geological Survey land cover categorization scheme based on a modified Anderson land-cover classification (U.S. Geol. Surv. 2007). Land area, tree canopy cover, and available green space within generalized land cover categories vary among communities, county subdivisions, counties, and state. The percentages are calculated from the NLCD 2001 and U.S. Census cartographic boundary data. The land-cover categories defined here are derived from established NLCD 2001 land-cover classes. These generalized land-cover categories or types may not be present in some states.

- Developed—NLCD classes 21 (developed-open space), 22 (developed-low intensity), 23 (developed-medium intensity), and 24 (developed-high intensity)
- Barren—NLCD class 31 (barren land [rock/sand/clay])
- Forested—NLCD classes 41 (deciduous forest), 42 (evergreen forest), and 43 (mixed forest)
- Shrub/Scrub—NLCD class 52 (shrub/scrub)
- Grassland—NLCD class 71 (grassland/herbaceous)
- Agriculture—NLCD classes 81 (pasture/hay) and 82 (cultivated crops)
- Wetland—NLCD classes 90 (woody wetlands) and 95 (emergent herbaceous wetlands).

For each state, Tables 8 through 10 summarize the classified land-cover characteristics for communities, county subdivisions, and counties and state respectively (http://www.nrs.fs.fed.us/data/urban).

Relative Comparisons of Urban and Community Forests

A question commonly asked in evaluating the urban and community forest resource is, "How does my community compare with other communities?"

To help answer this question, tree canopy cover was compared among the counties, county subdivisions, and communities relative to other areas with comparable population density and within the same NLCD mapping unit (ecoregion). For this comparison, seven population density classes were established:

- Density class 1 — 0 to 38.6 people/km^2 (0 to 99.9 people/mile^2),
- Density class 2 — 38.7 to 96.5 people/km^2 (100 to 249.9 people/mile^2),
- Density class 3 — 96.6 to 193.1 people/km^2 (250 to 499.9 people/mile^2),
- Density class 4 — 193.2 to 289.6 people/km^2 (500 to 749.9 people/mile^2),
- Density class 5 — 289.7 to 386.2 people/km^2 (750 to 999.9 people/mile^2),
- Density class 6 — 386.3 to 1931.2 people/km^2 (1000 to 4999.9 people/mile^2), and
- Density class 7— 1931.3 or greater people/km^2 (5000 or greater people/mile^2)

Mapping zones were delimited within the NLCD to increase classification accuracy and efficiency (Fig. A). The mapping units represent relatively homogeneous ecological conditions (Homer and Gallant 2001). To locate geopolitical units within a mapping zone, centroid (geometric center) points of the local governments were used.

For three or more geographic units in the same mapping zone and population density class, a standardized tree canopy score based on the range of values within that zone and class was assigned to each unit. The standardized score is calculated as:

Standardized score = (tree canopy percent of unit - minimum tree canopy percentage in class)/ range of tree canopy percent in class.

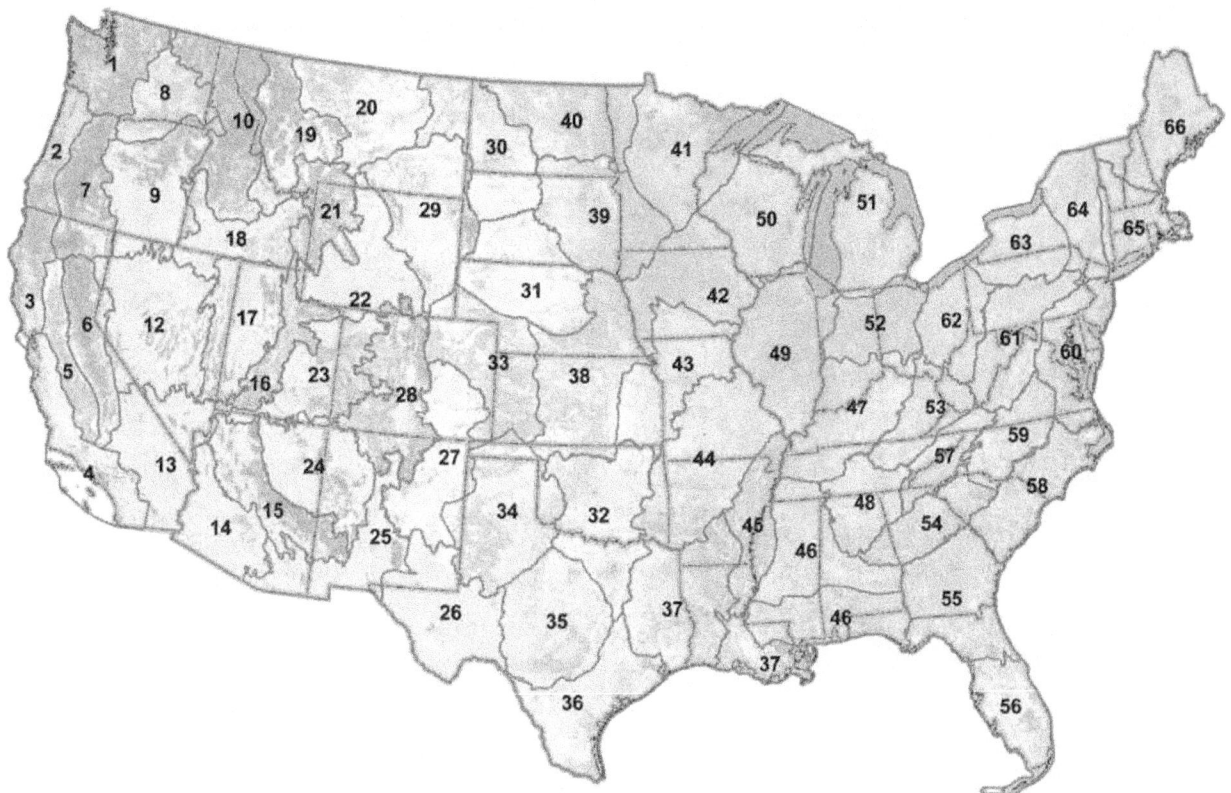

Figure A.—The mapping zones of the continental United States relative to states and land cover (NLCD 2001).

Communities, county subdivisions, and counties were assigned to one of the following categories based on their standardized score:

- Excellent—Standardized score of 0.9 to 1.0
- Very Good—0.7 to 0.89
- Good—0.5 to 0.69
- Fair—0.3 to 0.49
- Poor—0 to 0.29.

To help understand the variability of tree cover, minimum, median, maximum, and weighted mean values for percent tree canopy cover in each population density class of each political subdivision are reported in Table 11 for each mapping zone (CD and http://www.nrs.fs.fed.us/data/ urban). This information can be used to understand the actual range and values used for the assessment.

For each state, Tables 12 through 14 summarize the urban and community forest ratings for communities, county subdivisions, and counties respectively (CD and http://www.nrs.fs.fed.us/data/urban)

Priority Areas for Tree Planting

NLCD (U.S. Geol. Survey 2007) and 2000 U.S. Census data (2007) were used to produce an index that prioritizes tree planting areas for communities, county subdivisions, and counties. An index was developed to help identify areas with relatively low tree canopy cover and high population density (high priority tree-planting areas). This index provides one form of prioritization. States and local governments may design their own prioritization method incorporating individual and diverse value systems. The index used in this report combines three criteria.

- Population density—The greater the population density, the greater the priority for tree planting
- Canopy green space—The lower the value, the greater the priority for tree planting
- Tree canopy cover per capita—The lower the amount of tree canopy cover per person, the greater the priority for tree planting

Each criterion above was standardized[2] on a scale of 0 to 1, with 1 representing the maximum population density and minimum canopy green space and tree cover per capita. The standardized values were weighted to produce a combined score:

$$I = (PD * 40) + (CG * 30) + (TPC * 30)$$

Where I is the combined index score
PD is the standardized population density value
CG is the standardized canopy green space value, and
TPC is the standardized tree cover per capita value.

The combined score was standardized again and multiplied by 100 to produce the planting priority index. The tree planting priority index (PPI) ranks each state's communities, county subdivisions, and counties with values from 100 (highest priority) to 0 (lowest priority). This index is a type of "environmental equity" index with areas of higher human population density and lower canopy green space and tree cover per capita tending to get the higher index value.

For each state, Tables 15 through 17 summarize the tree planting priority index for communities, county subdivisions, and counties respectively (CD and http://www.nrs.fs.fed.us/data/urban)

Urban Tree Benefits

Urban and community forests are important for human and ecological health (Nowak and Dwyer 2007). The benefits ascribed to urban and community trees include:

_____

[2] Standardized value for population density (PD) was calculated as PD=(n-min)/r, where PD is the value 0-1, n is the value for the geopolitical unit (population/km^2), min is the minimum value for all units, and r is the range of values among all units (maximum value - minimum value). Standardized value for canopy green space (CG) was calculated as CG=(max-n)/r, where CG is the value 0-1, max is the maximum value for all geopolitical units, n is the value for the unit (tree canopy cover m^2/total green space m^2), and r is the range of values. Standardized value for tree cover per capita (TPC) was calculated as TPC=(max-n)/r, where TPC is the value (0-1), max is the maximum value for all geographic units, n is the value for the geopolitical unit (m^2/capita), and r is the range of values among all units.

- Carbon storage and sequestration
- Air pollution removal
- Surface air temperature reduction
- Reduced building energy use
- Absorption of ultraviolet radiation
- Improved water quality
- Reduced noise pollution
- Improved human comfort
- Increased property value
- Improved human physiological and psychological well-being
- Improved aesthetics
- Improved community cohesion

To understand the contribution and magnitude of the forest resource in urban or community areas, the total number of trees, carbon storage and annual carbon uptake (sequestration), air pollution removal, and the associated dollar values for carbon and air pollution benefits are estimated.

Carbon sequestration and storage values were estimated from tree cover (m^2) multiplied by average carbon storage (9.1 kg C/m^2), and sequestration (0.3 kg C/m^2) density values derived from several U.S. communities (e.g., Nowak and Crane 2002). Monetary values associated with urban tree carbon storage and sequestration were based on the 2001-2010 projected marginal social cost of carbon dioxide emissions, \$22.8/t C (Fankhauser 1994). The number of urban and community trees was estimated in a similar manner multiplying tree canopy cover (m^2) by average tree density per hectare of canopy cover from several U.S. cities (Table A).

Air pollution removal estimates are derived from the Urban Forest Effects (UFORE) model (Nowak and Crane 2000) and 2000 weather and pollution data (National Climatic Data Center 2000, U.S. EPA 2008). The UFORE model was used to integrate hourly pollution and weather data with urban or community tree cover data to estimate annual pollution removal in each state (Nowak and Crane 2000, Nowak et al. 2006d).

Table A.—Average number of trees, carbon storage, and carbon sequestration rates per unit of canopy cover for several U.S. cities

City	Trees (no./ha cover)	Carbon Storage (kg C/m^2 cover)	Carbon Sequestration (kg C/m^2 cover)
Atlanta, GA [a]	751.5	9.7	0.3
Baltimore, MD [a]	598.1	12.3	0.3
Boston, MA [a]	371.7	9.1	0.3
Chicago, IL [b]	618	12.9	n/a
Casper, WY [c]	252.8	7	0.2
Freehold, NJ [a]	275	10.4	0.3
Jersey City, NJ [a]	308.7	4.4	0.2
Minneapolis, MN [d]	245.5	5.7	0.2
Moorestown, NJ [a]	547.9	9.9	0.3
Morgantown, WV [a]	829.6	10.6	0.3
New York, NY [e]	312	7.3	0.2
Philadelphia, PA [f]	394.3	9	0.3
San Francisco, CA [g]	468.1	12.3	0.3
Syracuse, NY [h]	583.1	10.5	0.3
Oakland, CA [i]	570	5.2	n/a
Washington, DC [j]	423.4	10.4	0.3
Woodbridge, NJ [a]	557.3	8.2	0.3
Mean	476.9	9.1	0.3

[a] Unpublished data analyzed using UFORE model
[b] Nowak 1994a,b
[c] Nowak et al. 2006a
[d] Nowak et al. 2006b
[e] Nowak et al. 2007a
[f] Nowak et al. 2007b
[g] Nowak et al. 2007c
[h] Nowak et al. 2001a
[i] Nowak 1993; Nowak and Crane 2002
[j] Nowak et al. 2006c

To estimate pollution by urban trees in each state, state pollutant flux rates (grams of pollution removal per square meter of canopy per year) were derived from a study of national pollution removal by urban trees for the year 1994 (Nowak et al. 2006d). As pollution concentrations vary through time, the 1994 flux rates were adjusted to 2000 values based on average regional pollution concentration changes between 1994 and 2000 (U.S. EPA 2003). As

flux rate = deposition velocity * pollution concentration,

the ratio of the pollution concentration between years was used to update the flux rate. Arithmetic mean concentration values were used for nitrogen dioxide, particulate matter less than 10 microns, and sulfur dioxide, 2nd Max. 8-hr average for carbon dioxide, and 4th Max. 8-hr average for ozone, to determine the ratio

of change between 1994 and 2000 (U.S. EPA 2003). The new 2000 flux rates were multiplied by urban or community tree cover in the state to estimate total pollution removal by trees.

Pollution removal dollar value estimates were calculated using 1994 national median externality values used in energy decision making (Murray et al. 1994, Ottinger et al. 1990). The 1994 values were adjusted to 2007 dollars based on the producer price index (U.S. Dept. of Labor 2008). These values, in dollars/metric ton (t) are:

- Nitrogen dioxide (NO_2) = $9,906/t
- Particulate matter less than 10 microns (PM_{10}) = $6,614/t
- Sulfur dioxide (SO_2) = $2,425/t
- Carbon monoxide (CO) = $1,407/t

Externality values for ozone (O_3) were set to equal the value for NO_2. Externality values can be considered the estimated cost of pollution to society that is not accounted for in the market price of the goods or services that produced the pollution.

For each state, Table 1 summarizes carbon storage and air pollution removal estimates for urban, community, and urban or community trees statewide.

Data Accuracy and Application

The data presented in this report yield the most comprehensive and up-to-date assessment of continental U.S. urban and community forests. The data allows for relative comparisons among geographies and provides baseline information for assessing relative changes in urban and community forest cover in the future. As stated previously, tree cover information was based on finer resolution data than used in the original urban forest assessment (Dwyer et al. 2000). As the methodologies for quantifying tree cover have changed between the original and current assessment, evaluating changes is not possible since the detected changes could be caused by either actual landscape changes or differences in methodology.

The U.S. Census generalized cartographic boundary data are a simplified and smoothed extracts of the Topologically Integrated Geographic Encoding and Referencing (TIGER) database, with a target scale range of 1:5,000,000 (U.S. Census Bureau 2007). Because of this scale and generalization, border simplification impacts attribute measurements that are derived from the boundary data, especially for small areas and at the local scale. In particular, percentages (unitless ratios) generated from attribute measurements made for the smallest Communities or County Subdivisions may be under- or overstated depending upon the relative location of the smoothed border of the geopolitical unit.

While the 2001 NLCD is a substantial improvement over the 1991 AVHRR data (30-m versus 1-km resolution), it also has local-scale data and application limitations. Initial tree canopy cover results revealed mean absolute errors (mean of the absolute difference

between predicted and actual values) from 8.4 percent to 14.1 percent, with correlation coefficients between predicted and actual values ranging from 0.78 to 0.93. Impervious surface cover results revealed mean absolute errors from 4.6 percent to 7 percent, with r-values from 0.83 to 0.91 (Homer et al. 2004).

A more recent analysis of 127 community and 20 county geographies sampled throughout the continental United States compared NLCD tree canopy and impervious surface cover estimates with high resolution (1-m or less resolution) aerial photo-interpreted estimates. This analysis revealed that NLCD underestimates both tree canopy and impervious surface cover compared to photo-interpreted values. NLCD underestimates of tree cover vary by mapping zone, while underestimates of impervious surface cover, which are relatively minor, varies by population density[3]. These findings are consistent with Walton (2008), who found a consistent under-prediction bias for the 2001 NLCD derived tree canopy cover values in census places (communities) of western New York.

The tree cover and impervious cover data given in this report are directly from the NLCD database. To help understand the potential underestimate in the cover values, each U.S. mapping zone was photo-interpreted using Google Earth images. Table B provides a comparison of results from NLCD versus photo-interpreted data for mapping zones applicable to this collection of states.

Comparisons between NLCD impervious surface cover estimates and photo-interpreted values were not reported because differences were related to population density, which can vary significantly among geographic units. Despite the potential underestimates in tree canopy cover values, relative comparisons of tree cover among geographies in this report (e.g. planting priority index and the ratings of excellent to poor for local government tree cover) are reasonable as the under-prediction of

---

[3]Greenfield, E.J.; Nowak D.J.; Walton, J.T. Assessment of 2001 NLCD percent tree and impervious cover estimates. In review.

Table B.—Comparison of NLCD versus photo-interpretation (PI) derived values of percent tree canopy cover by NLCD mapping zones

Mapping zone [a]	n [b]	Percent tree canopy cover		Difference [e]	Margin of error [f]	Significant difference [g]
		NLCD [c]	PI [d]			
66	581	69.6%	84.9%	15.3%	2.9%	Yes
65	938	62.6%	71.1%	8.5%	2.9%	Yes

[a] NLCD mapping zones

[b] Number of photo-interpreted sample points

[c] Percent tree canopy value derived from NLCD data

[d] Percent tree canopy derived from photo-interpreted data

[e] PI value minus NLCD value

[f] 95% confidence interval of PI value

[g] Significant difference between NLCD and PI values if NLCD value is outside of 95% confidence interval of PI value

tree cover is fairly consistent within each mapping zone. However, it is important to note that the tree canopy and impervious surface cover could be underestimated, as well as their associated ecosystem services and values. A forthcoming analysis will better assess the accuracy of the NLCD cover maps (Homer et al. 2007), but these maps and data provide comprehensive, consistent, and comparable estimates (with an inherent degree of error and uncertainty) of tree canopy and impervious surface cover to help urban and community forest management, planning and policy making. Higher resolution cover data may provide more accurate results at the local scale, but the NLCD cover maps provide a cost-effective means to consistently assess and compare the relative differences of urban cover types regionally. For more refined and locally appropriate data, local field or high resolution (1 m or less) image analyses are recommended (e.g., i-Tree www.itreetools.org; UTC – www.nrs.fs.fed.us/urban/utc).

Because of limited urban and community forest field data, data from several urban and community forests were used to estimate the number of trees and carbon storage by trees. These coarse estimates reveal that urban and community forests contain a large number of trees and provide significant environmental benefits. Field data are needed from all states to help improve these estimates as well as to estimate other forest effects (e.g., building energy conservation and changes in stream flow and water quality). Data from long-term monitoring of urban and community forests used in conjunction with satellite-based cover maps will provide essential information to assess forest health and change, and to improve urban and community forest management.

Practical Applications for Managers

The data from this report can be used to aid urban forest management at both the state and local levels. Data can be used to:

- Determine the extent, magnitude, and variation in the urban and community forestry resource
- Determine areas of greatest population growth, urbanization, and development (sprawl) to direct urban and community forestry to minimize negative impacts and maximize environmental benefits
- Evaluate existing tree canopy, impervious surface cover, and available planting space (available green space) to direct current and future urban and community forestry efforts such as planting programs
- Compare tree canopy cover for similar geopolitical units and set tree canopy goals
- Prioritize tree planting based on population density, tree canopy green space, and tree canopy cover per person
- Understand the pollution removal and carbon storage benefits of urban and community forests

- Promote more detailed and/or locally appropriate urban and community forest inventories, censuses, or field surveys (e.g. i-Tree - www.itreetools.org)
- Establish statewide to local standards related to urban and community forestry (e.g., establishing minimum goals of percent canopy green space or tree cover per capita and directing resources so that communities can reach the minimum standards)
- Improve urban and community forest management and cost estimation by providing an estimate of the number of trees in each geopolitical unit (i.e., urban area size (ha) * percent tree cover * 477 trees/ha, or local tree density information from local data).
- Guide policy decisions related to urban sprawl and urban and community forest management.

SUMMARY

The data presented in this report provide a better understanding of urban and community forests. This information can be used to advance urban and community forest policy and management that could improve environmental quality and human health throughout the state. The following sections detail specific urban and community forestry data for the states in this regional report.

ACKNOWLEDGMENTS

This research was funded, in part, by the U.S. Forest Service, RPA Assessment Staff, and Northeastern Area State and Private Forestry's Urban and Community Forestry Program. Thanks also goes to State University of New York College of Environmental Science and Forestry Research Assistant Nana Efua Imbeah for assistance with data processing.

CONNECTICUT'S URBAN AND COMMUNITY FORESTS

Summary

Urban or community land in Connecticut comprises about 39.9 percent of the state land area in 2000, an increase from 35.8 percent in 1990. Statewide tree canopy cover averages 64.5 percent and tree cover in urban or community areas is about 51.0 percent, with 15.4 percent impervious surface cover and 60.3 percent of the total green space covered by tree canopy cover. Statewide, urban or community land has an estimated 121.9 million trees, which store about 23.3 million metric tons of carbon ($531.2 million), and annually remove about 767,000 metric tons of carbon ($17.5 million) and 17,380 metric tons of air pollution ($145.1 million) (Table CT-1).

Tables CT-2 through CT-17 are not printed in this report but are available on the CD located on the inside back cover, and at http://www.nrs.fs.fed.us/data/urban.

Table CT-1.—Statewide summary of population, area, population density, tree canopy and impervious surface land cover, and urban tree benefits in urban, community, and urban or community areas.

Connecticut		Statewide	Urban [a]	Community [b]	Urban or community [c]
Population	2000	3,405,565	2,988,059	2,029,172	n/a
	1990	3,287,116	2,601,548	1,940,568	n/a
	% Change (1990-2000)	3.6	14.9	4.6	n/a
	% Total population (2000)	100.0	87.7	59.6	n/a
Total area	km² (2000)	14,357.2	4,655.6	2,500.5	5,148.9
	km² (1990)	14,357.2	4,060.3	2,469.3	4,598.5
	% Change (1990-2000)	0.0	14.7	1.3	12.0
Land area	km² (2000)	12,540.8	4,561.5	2,410.6	5,009.5
	% Land area (2000)	100.0	36.4	19.2	39.9
	km² (1990)	12,540.8	4,008.1	2,384.4	4,485.5
	% Land area (1990)	100.0	32.0	19.0	35.8
	% Change (1990-2000)	0.0	13.8	1.1	11.7
Population density (people/land area km²)	2000	271.6	655.1	841.8	n/a
	1990	262.1	649.1	813.8	n/a
	% Change (1990-2000)	3.6	0.9	3.4	n/a
Tree canopy cover (2000)	km²	8,094.8	2,248.4	1,091.4	2,556.0
	% Land area	64.5	49.3	45.3	51.0
	Per capita (m²/person)	2,376.9	752.5	537.8	n/a
	% Canopy green space [d]	69.4	59.1	57.3	60.3
Total green space (2000) [e]	km²	11,667.2	3,801.9	1,903.6	4,237.0
	% Land area	93.0	83.3	79.0	84.6
Available green space (2000) [f]	km²	3,573.7	1,554.4	812.8	1,682.0
	% Land area	28.5	34.1	33.7	33.6
Impervious surface cover (2000)	km²	873.6	759.6	507.0	772.5
	% Land area	7.0	16.7	21.0	15.4
	Per capita (m²/person)	256.5	254.2	249.8	n/a
Urban tree benefits (2000)	Estimated number of trees	n/a	107,200,000	52,000,000	121,900,000
	Carbon				
	Carbon stored (metric tons)	n/a	20,500,000	9,900,000	23,300,000
	Carbon stored ($)	n/a	$467,400,000	$225,700,000	$531,200,000
	Carbon sequestered (metric tons/year)	n/a	675,000	327,000	767,000
	Carbon sequestered ($/year)	n/a	$15,390,000	$7,456,000	$17,488,000
	Pollution				
	CO removed (metric tons/year)	n/a	368	179	419
	CO removed ($/year)	n/a	$518,200	$251,500	$589,100
	NO₂ removed (metric tons/year)	n/a	2,500	1,213	2,842
	NO₂ removed ($/year)	n/a	$24,761,800	$12,019,600	$28,149,300
	O₃ removed (metric tons/year)	n/a	7,367	3,576	8,375
	O₃ removed ($/year)	n/a	$72,982,000	$35,426,000	$82,966,000
	SO₂ removed (metric tons/year)	n/a	976	474	1,110
	SO₂ removed ($/year)	n/a	$2,367,600	$1,149,200	$2,691,400
	PM₁₀ removed (metric tons/year)	n/a	4,079	1,980	4,638
	PM₁₀ removed ($/year)	n/a	$26,981,700	$13,097,100	$30,672,800
	Total pollution removal (metric tons/year)	n/a	15,290	7,420	17,380
	Total pollution removal ($/year)	n/a	$127,600,000	$61,900,000	$145,100,000

[a] Urban land is based on population density and was delimited using the U.S. Census definitions of urbanized areas and urban clusters. [b] Community land is based on jurisdictional or political boundaries of communities based on U.S. Census definitions of incorporated or census designated places. [c] Urban or communities is land that is urban, community, or both. Communities may include all, some, or no urban land within their boundaries. [d] Canopy green space is the tree canopy cover divided by total green space. [e] Total green space is total area minus impervious surface cover minus water. [f] Available green space is total green space minus tree canopy cover (if the calculated value is less than 0, then value set at 0).

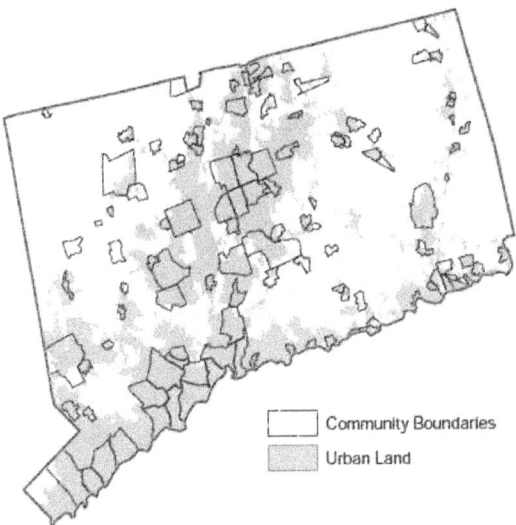

Figure CT-1.—Urban or community land in 2000; urban area relative to community boundaries.

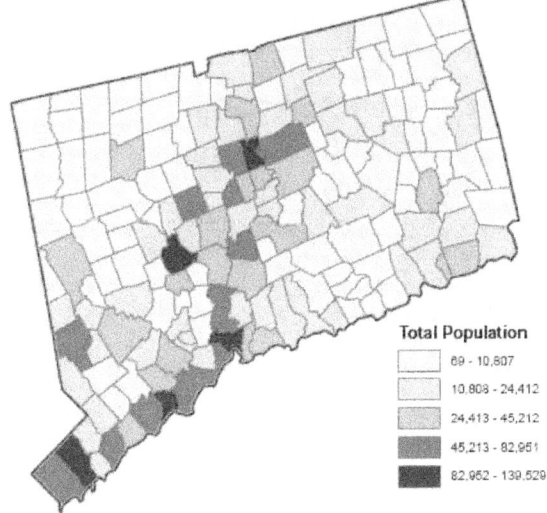

Figure CT-2.—2000 Population within county subdivision boundaries.

Human Population Characteristics and Trends

The population in Connecticut increased 3.6 percent, from 3,287,116 in 1990 to 3,405,565 in 2000 (Table CT-1). In Connecticut, 87.7 percent of the state's population is in urban areas (Fig. CT-1), and 59.6 percent of the population is within communities (Fig. CT-2).

Urban and Community Land

Urban land comprises 36.4 percent of the land area of Connecticut, while lands within communities make up 19.2 percent of the state (Fig. CT-1). Between 1990 and 2000, urban area increased 13.8 percent, while community land increased from 19.0 to 19.2 percent (Table CT-1). Urban area in Connecticut is projected to increase to 60.9 percent by 2050, based on average urban growth pattern of the 1990s (Nowak and Walton 2005). Both urban land (attaining minimum population density) and community land (political boundaries) increased from 1990 to 2000. The percentages are calculated using the total (water and land) area of the geopolitical units derived from U.S. Census cartographic boundary data. Percent urban land varied across the state (Fig. CT-3; Tables CT-2 through 4).

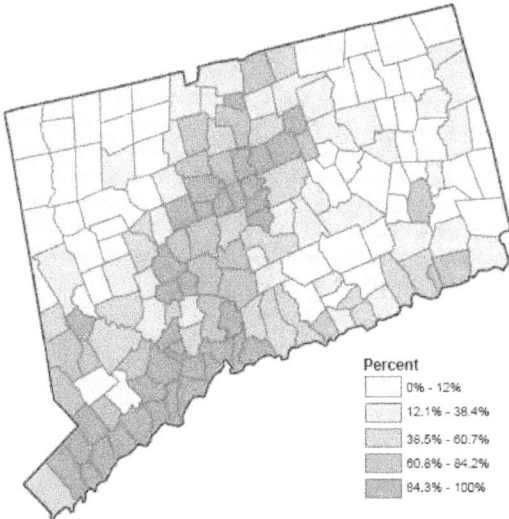

Figure CT-3.—Percent of community subdivision area classified as urban land in 2000.

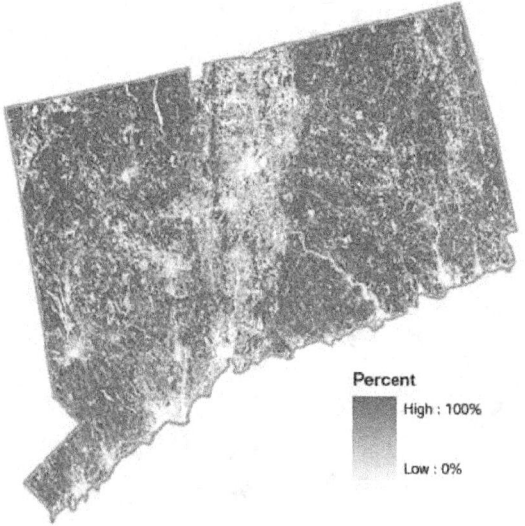

Figure CT-4.—Percentage tree canopy cover.

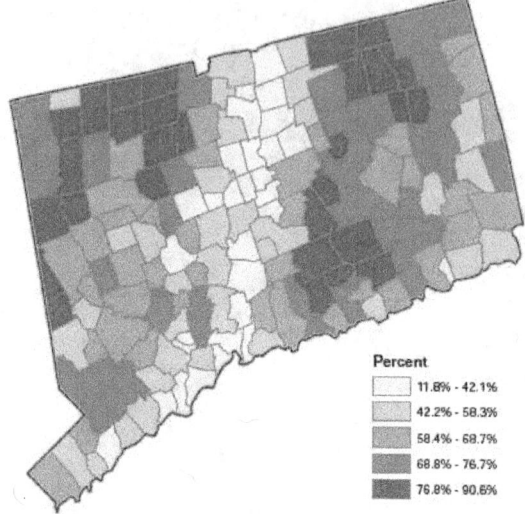

Percent
11.8% - 42.1%
42.2% - 58.3%
58.4% - 68.7%
68.8% - 76.7%
76.8% - 90.6%

Figure CT-5.—Percentage tree canopy cover within county subdivisions.

Tree Canopy Cover Characteristics

Tree canopy cover in Connecticut averages 64.5 percent (Fig. CT-4), with 93.0 percent total green space, 69.4 percent canopy green space, and 2,376.9 m^2 of canopy cover per capita. Average tree cover in urban areas in Connecticut was 49.3 percent, with 83.3 percent total green space, 59.1 percent canopy green space, and 752.5 m^2 of canopy cover per capita. Within community lands in Connecticut, average tree cover was 45.3 percent, with 79.0 percent total green space, 57.3 percent canopy green space, and 537.8 m^2 of canopy cover per capita (Table CT-1). Tree canopy cover, canopy green space, and tree cover per capita varied among communities, county subdivisions, and counties (Fig. CT-5 through 6; Tables CT-5 through 7).

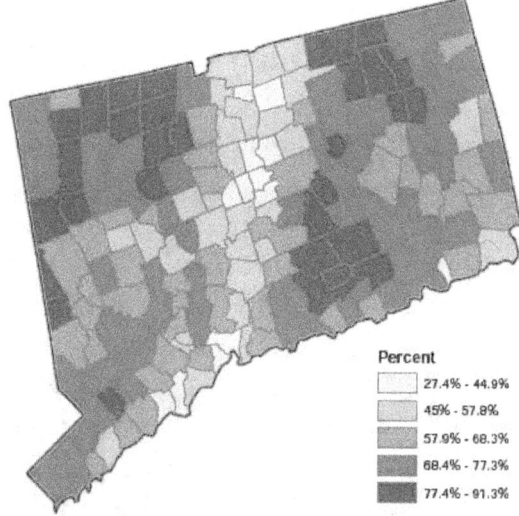

Percent
27.4% - 44.9%
45% - 57.8%
57.9% - 68.3%
68.4% - 77.3%
77.4% - 91.3%

Figure CT-6.—Percentage tree canopy green space in county subdivisions.

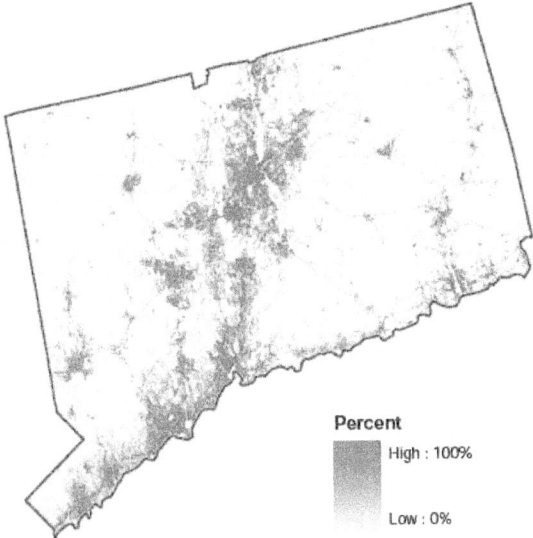

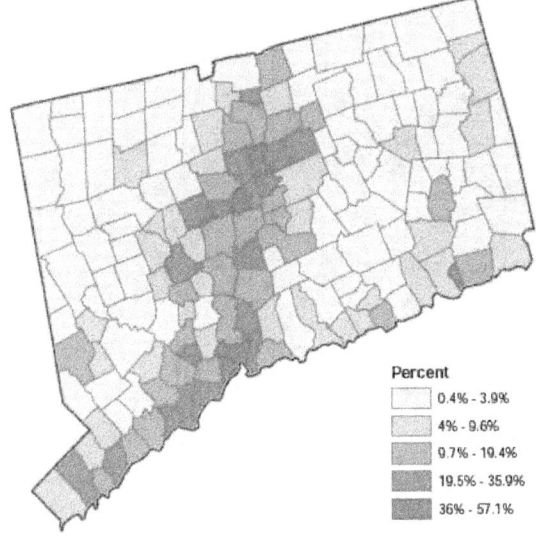

Figure CT-7.—Percentage impervious surface cover.

Figure CT-8.—Percentage impervious surface cover within county subdivisions.

Impervious Surface Cover Characteristics

Average impervious surface cover in Connecticut is 7.0 percent of the land area (Fig. CT-7), with 256.5 m^2 of impervious surface cover per capita. Average impervious surface cover in urban areas was 16.7 percent, with 254.2 m^2 of impervious surface cover per capita. Within community lands in Connecticut, average impervious surface cover was 21.0 percent with 249.8 m^2 of impervious surface cover per capita (Table CT-1). Impervious surface cover varied across the state (Fig. CT-8; Tables CT-5 through 7).

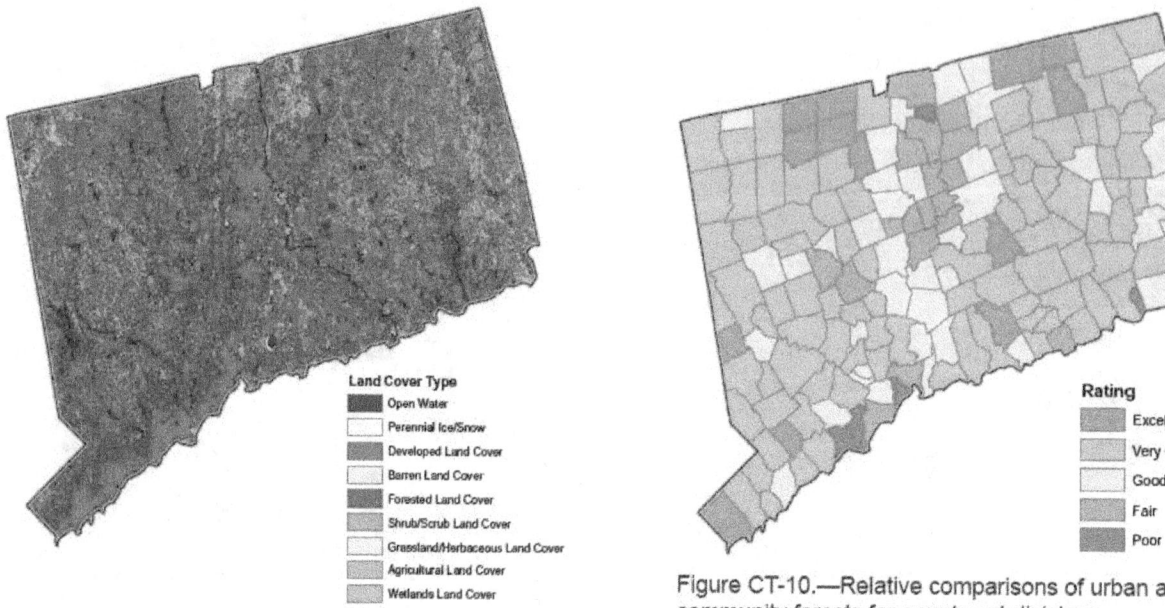

Land Cover Type
- Open Water
- Perennial Ice/Snow
- Developed Land Cover
- Barren Land Cover
- Forested Land Cover
- Shrub/Scrub Land Cover
- Grassland/Herbaceous Land Cover
- Agricultural Land Cover
- Wetlands Land Cover

Figure CT-9.—Classified land cover.

Rating
- Excellent
- Very Good
- Good
- Fair
- Poor

Figure CT-10.—Relative comparisons of urban and community forests for county subdivisions.

Classified Land-cover Characteristics

Connecticut's landcover is dominated by forest land (Fig. CT-9). The characteristics as a percent of the total land area in Connecticut are (Tables CT-8 through 10):

- Forested—58.2 percent
- Developed—23.7 percent
- Agricultural—15.4 percent
- Scrub/Shrub—1.3 percent
- Wetland—0.8 percent
- Grassland—0.3 percent
- Barren—0.3 percent

Relative Comparisons of Urban and Community Forests

Out of the 120 Connecticut communities, four received a rating of excellent and 14 received a rating of poor (Table CT-12). Of the 169 county subdivisions, 13 had a rating of excellent and five were rated poor (Fig. CT-10, Table CT-13); and out of eight counties, none were given a rating of excellent or poor (Table CT-14). Variability of assessment scores is a product of the difference in land cover distributions and the percentage of canopy cover within the population density classes and mapping zones (Fig CT-10; Tables CT-11 through 14).

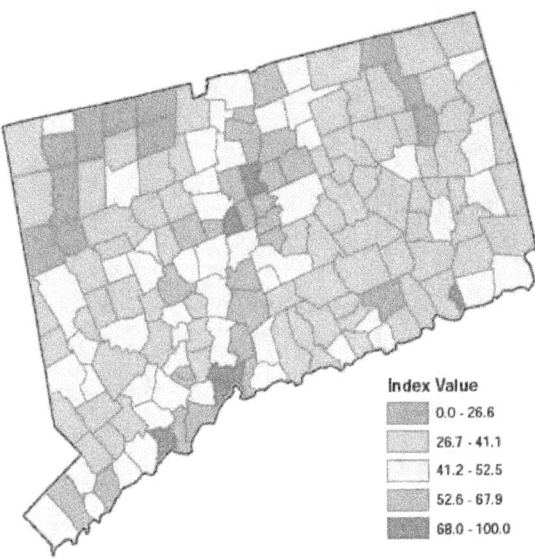

Index Value
- 0.0 - 26.6
- 26.7 - 41.1
- 41.2 - 52.5
- 52.6 - 67.9
- 68.0 - 100.0

Figure CT-11.—Planting priority index for county subdivisions. The higher the index value, the greater priority for planting.

Priority Areas for Tree Planting

Priority areas for planting tend to be highest in more urbanized areas due to higher population density (Fig. CT-11; Tables CT-15 through 17). These index values can also be produced using high resolution cover data to determine local planting priority areas (e.g., neighborhoods).

Urban Tree Benefits

The following forest attributes are estimated for the urban or community land in Connecticut (Table CT-1). These are rough estimates of values. More localized data are needed for more precise estimates, but these values reveal first-order approximations.

- 121.9 million trees
- 23.3 million metric tons of C stored ($531.2 million value)
- 767,000 metric tons/year of C sequestered ($17.5 million value)
- 17,380 metric tons/year total pollution removal ($145.1 million value)
  - 419 metric tons/year of CO removed ($589,100 value)
  - 2,842 metric tons/year NO_2 removed ($28.1 million value)
  - 8,375 metric tons/year of O_3 removed ($83.0 million value)
  - 1,110 metric tons/year of SO_2 removed ($2.7 million value)
  - 4,638 metric tons/year of PM_{10} removed ($30.7 million value).

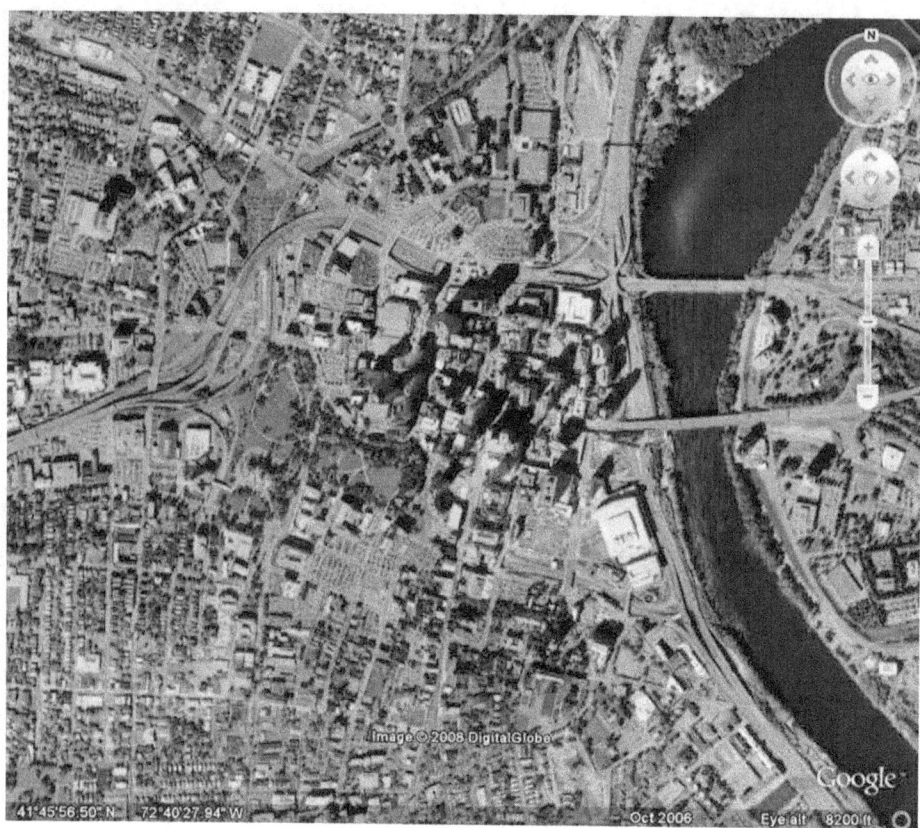

Summary

The data presented in this report provide a better understanding of Connecticut's urban and community forests. This information can be used to advance urban and community forestry policy and management that could improve environmental quality and human health throughout the state.

These data establish a baseline to assess future change and can be used to understand:

- Extent of the urban and community forest resource
- Variations in the resource across the state
- Magnitude and value of the urban and community forest resource
- Urban growth in Connecticut
- Implications of policy decisions related to urban sprawl and urban and community forest management

MAINE'S URBAN AND COMMUNITY FORESTS

Summary

Urban or community land in Maine comprises about 4.2 percent of the state land area in 2000, an increase from 4.0 percent in 1990. Statewide tree canopy cover averages 69.1 percent and tree cover in urban or community areas is about 46.7 percent, with 7.8 percent impervious surface cover and 50.6 percent of the total green space covered by tree canopy cover. Statewide, urban or community land in Maine has an estimated 74.9 million trees, which store about 14.3 million metric tons of carbon ($326 million), and annually remove about 471,000 metric tons of carbon ($10.7 million) and 8,670 metric tons of air pollution ($74.1 million) (Table ME-1).

Tables ME-2 through ME-17 are not printed in this report but are available on the CD located on the inside back cover, and at http://www.nrs.fs.fed.us/data/urban.

Table ME-1.—Statewide summary of population, area, population density, tree canopy and impervious surface land cover, and urban tree benefits in urban, community, and urban or community areas.

Maine		Statewide	Urban [a]	Community [b]	Urban or community [c]
Population	2000	1,274,923	512,878	597,613	n/a
	1990	1,227,928	547,824	611,386	n/a
	% Change (1990-2000)	3.8	-6.4	-2.3	n/a
	% Total population (2000)	100.0	40.2	46.9	n/a
Total area	km² (2000)	91,645.8	927.7	3,330.2	3,592.8
	km² (1990)	91,645.8	854.0	3,172.2	3,375.1
	% Change (1990-2000)	0.0	8.6	5.0	6.5
Land area	km² (2000)	80,167.5	910.8	3,111.3	3,367.0
	% Land area (2000)	100.0	1.1	3.9	4.2
	km² (1990)	80,167.5	845.9	2,970.3	3,170.8
	% Land area (1990)	100.0	1.1	3.7	4.0
	% Change (1990-2000)	0.0	7.7	4.7	6.2
Population density (people/land area km²)	2000	15.9	563.1	192.1	n/a
	1990	15.3	647.6	205.8	n/a
	% Change (1990-2000)	3.8	-13.0	-6.7	n/a
Tree canopy cover (2000)	km²	55,419.1	309.7	1,469.4	1,571.4
	% Land area	69.1	34.0	47.2	46.7
	Per capita (m²/person)	43,468.6	603.8	2,458.8	n/a
	% Canopy green space [d]	69.7	41.5	51.2	50.6
Total green space (2000) [e]	km²	79,546.3	745.7	2,868.6	3,105.2
	% Land area	99.2	81.9	92.2	92.2
Available green space (2000) [f]	km²	24,128.2	436.1	1,399.3	1,534.0
	% Land area	30.1	47.9	45.0	45.6
Impervious surface cover (2000)	km²	621.2	165.1	242.7	261.7
	% Land area	0.8	18.1	7.8	7.8
	Per capita (m²/person)	487.3	321.8	406.2	n/a
	Estimated number of trees	n/a	14,800,000	70,100,000	74,900,000
	Carbon				
	Carbon stored (metric tons)	n/a	2,800,000	13,400,000	14,300,000
	Carbon stored ($)	n/a	$63,800,000	$305,500,000	$326,000,000
	Carbon sequestered (metric tons/year)	n/a	93,000	441,000	471,000
	Carbon sequestered ($/year)	n/a	$2,120,000	$10,055,000	$10,739,000
	Pollution				
Urban tree benefits (2000)	CO removed (metric tons/year)	n/a	27	126	135
	CO removed ($/year)	n/a	$37,400	$177,600	$189,900
	NO₂ removed (metric tons/year)	n/a	164	778	832
	NO₂ removed ($/year)	n/a	$1,624,500	$7,708,100	$8,242,900
	O₃ removed (metric tons/year)	n/a	993	4,713	5,040
	O₃ removed ($/year)	n/a	$9,839,000	$46,683,000	$49,922,000
	SO₂ removed (metric tons/year)	n/a	87	415	443
	SO₂ removed ($/year)	n/a	$211,800	$1,005,200	$1,074,900
	PM₁₀ removed (metric tons/year)	n/a	437	2,073	2,217
	PM₁₀ removed ($/year)	n/a	$2,889,500	$13,710,200	$14,661,400
	Total pollution removal (metric tons/year)	n/a	1,710	8,100	8,670
	Total pollution removal ($/year)	n/a	$14,600,000	$69,300,000	$74,100,000

[a] Urban land is based on population density and was delimited using the U.S. Census definitions of urbanized areas and urban clusters. [b] Community land is based on jurisdictional or political boundaries of communities based on U.S. Census definitions of incorporated or census designated places. [c] Urban or communities is land that is urban, community, or both. Communities may include all, some, or no urban land within their boundaries. [d] Canopy green space is the tree canopy cover divided by total green space. [e] Total green space is total area minus impervious surface cover minus water. [f] Available green space is total green space minus tree canopy cover (if the calculated value is less than 0, then value set at 0).

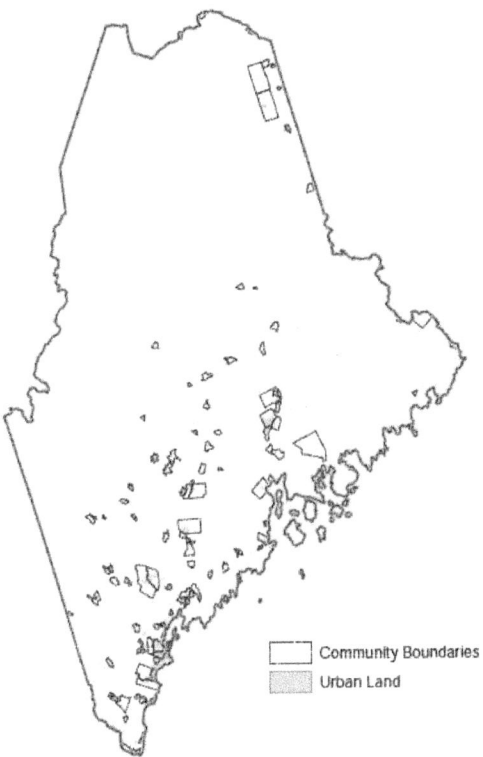

Figure ME-1.—Urban or community land in 2000; urban area relative to community boundaries.

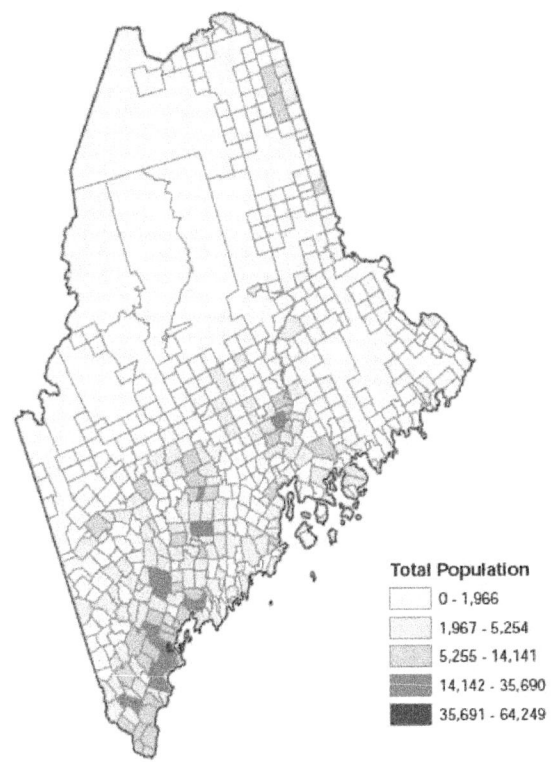

Figure ME-2.—2000 Population within county subdivision boundaries.

Human Population Characteristics and Trends

The population in Maine increased 3.8 percent, from 1,227,928 in 1990 to 1,274,923 in 2000 (Table ME-1). In Maine, 40.2 percent of the state's population is in urban areas (Fig. ME-1), and 46.9 percent of the population is within communities (Fig. ME-2).

Urban and Community Land

Urban land comprises 1.1 percent of the land area of Maine, while lands within communities make up 3.9 percent of the state (Fig. ME-1). Between 1990 and 2000, urban area increased slightly, while community land increased from 3.7 to 3.9 percent (Table ME-1). Urban area in Maine is projected to increase to 3.8 percent by 2050, based on average urban growth pattern of the 1990s (Nowak and Walton 2005). Both urban land (attaining minimum population density) and community land (political boundaries) increased from 1990 to 2000. The percentages are calculated using the total (water and land) area of the geopolitical units derived from U.S. Census cartographic boundary data. Percent urban land varied across the state (Fig. ME-3; Tables ME-2 through 4).

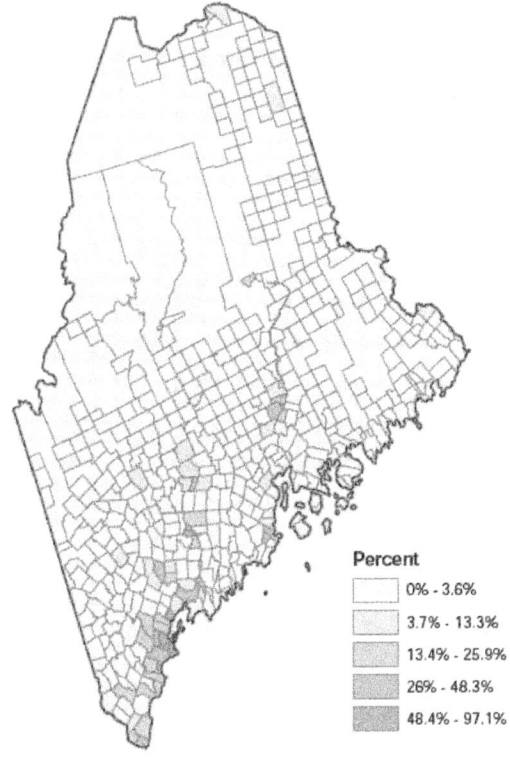

Figure ME-3.—Percent of community subdivision area classified as urban land in 2000.

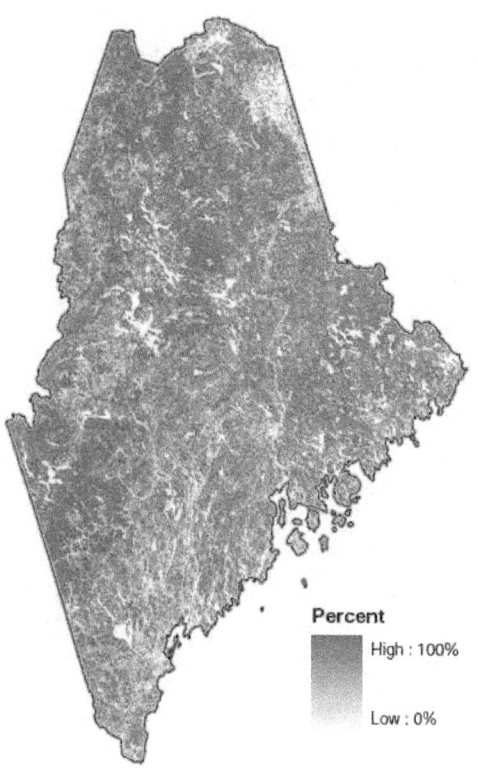

Figure ME-4.—Percentage tree canopy cover.

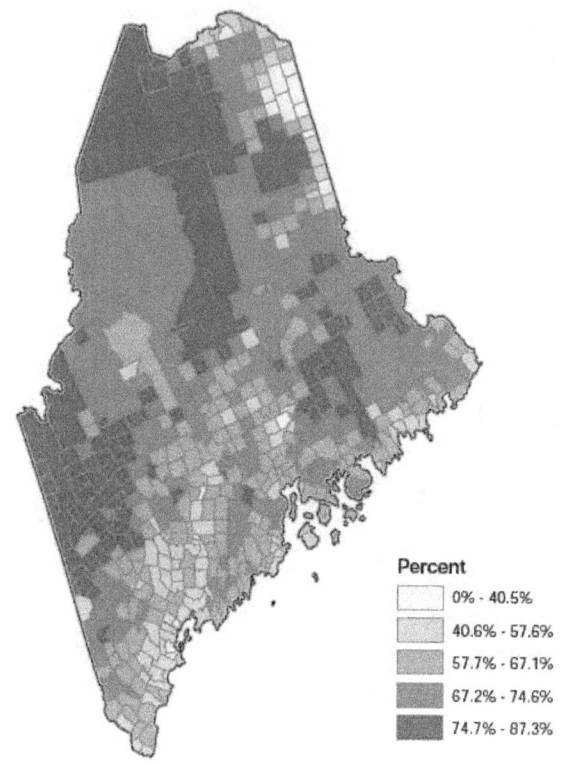

Percent
- 0% - 40.5%
- 40.6% - 57.6%
- 57.7% - 67.1%
- 67.2% - 74.6%
- 74.7% - 87.3%

Figure ME-5.—Percentage tree canopy cover within county subdivisions.

Tree Canopy Cover Characteristics

Tree canopy cover in Maine averages 69.1 percent (Fig. ME-4), with 99.2 percent total green space, 69.7 percent canopy green space, and 43,468.6 m^2 of canopy cover per capita. Average tree cover in urban areas in Maine was 34.0 percent, with 81.9 percent total green space, 41.5 percent canopy green space, and 603.8 m^2 of canopy cover per capita. Within community lands in Maine, average tree cover was 47.2 percent, with 92.2 percent total green space, 51.2 percent canopy green space, and 2,458.8 m^2 of canopy cover per capita (Table ME-1). Tree canopy cover, canopy green space, and tree cover per capita varied among communities, county subdivisions, and counties (Fig. ME-5 through 6; Tables ME-5 through 7).

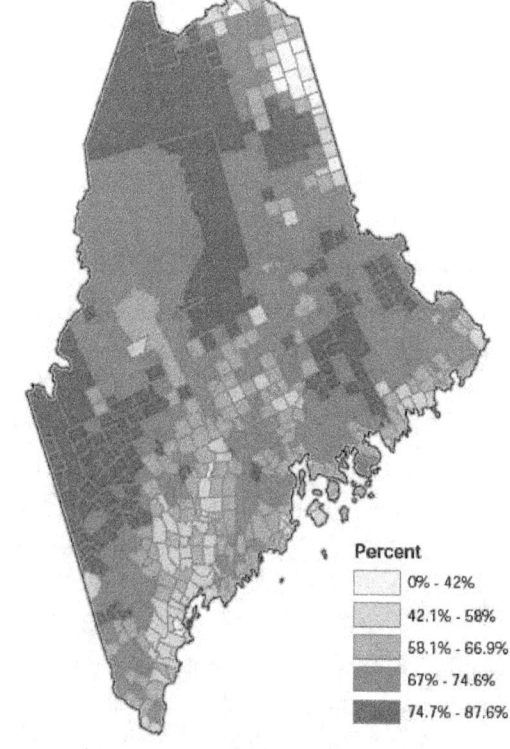

Percent
- 0% - 42%
- 42.1% - 58%
- 58.1% - 66.9%
- 67% - 74.6%
- 74.7% - 87.6%

Figure ME-6.—Percentage tree canopy green space in county subdivisions.

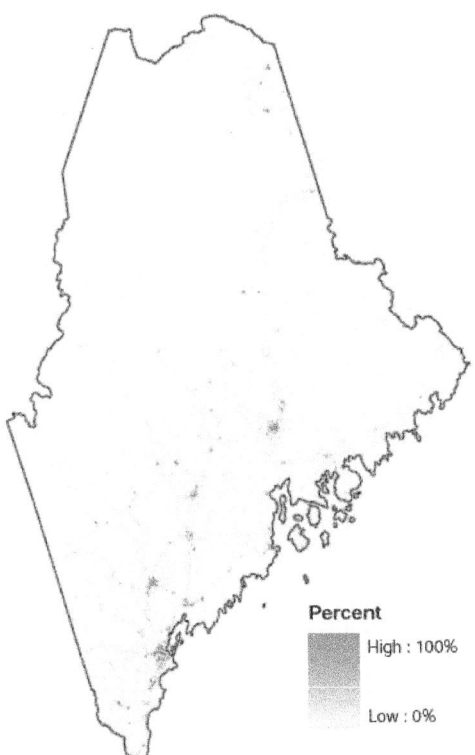

Percent

High : 100%

Low : 0%

Figure ME-7. —Percentage impervious surface cover.

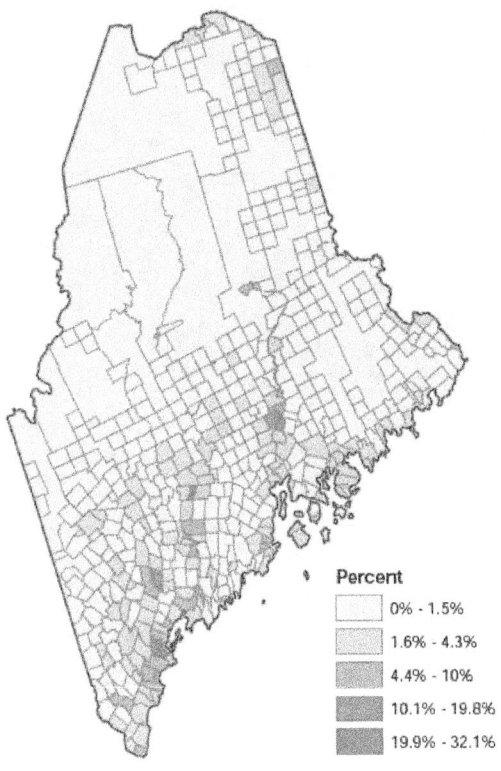

Percent

	0% - 1.5%
	1.6% - 4.3%
	4.4% - 10%
	10.1% - 19.8%
	19.9% - 32.1%

Figure ME-8.—Percentage impervious surface cover within county subdivisions.

Impervious Surface Cover Characteristics

Average impervious surface cover in Maine is 0.8 percent of the land area (Fig. ME-7), with 487.3 m^2 of impervious surface cover per capita. Average impervious surface cover in urban areas was 18.1 percent, with 321.8 m^2 of impervious surface cover per capita. Within community lands in Maine, average impervious surface cover was 7.8 percent with 406.2 m^2 of impervious surface cover per capita (Table ME-1). Impervious surface cover varied across the state (Fig. ME-8; Tables ME-5 through 7).

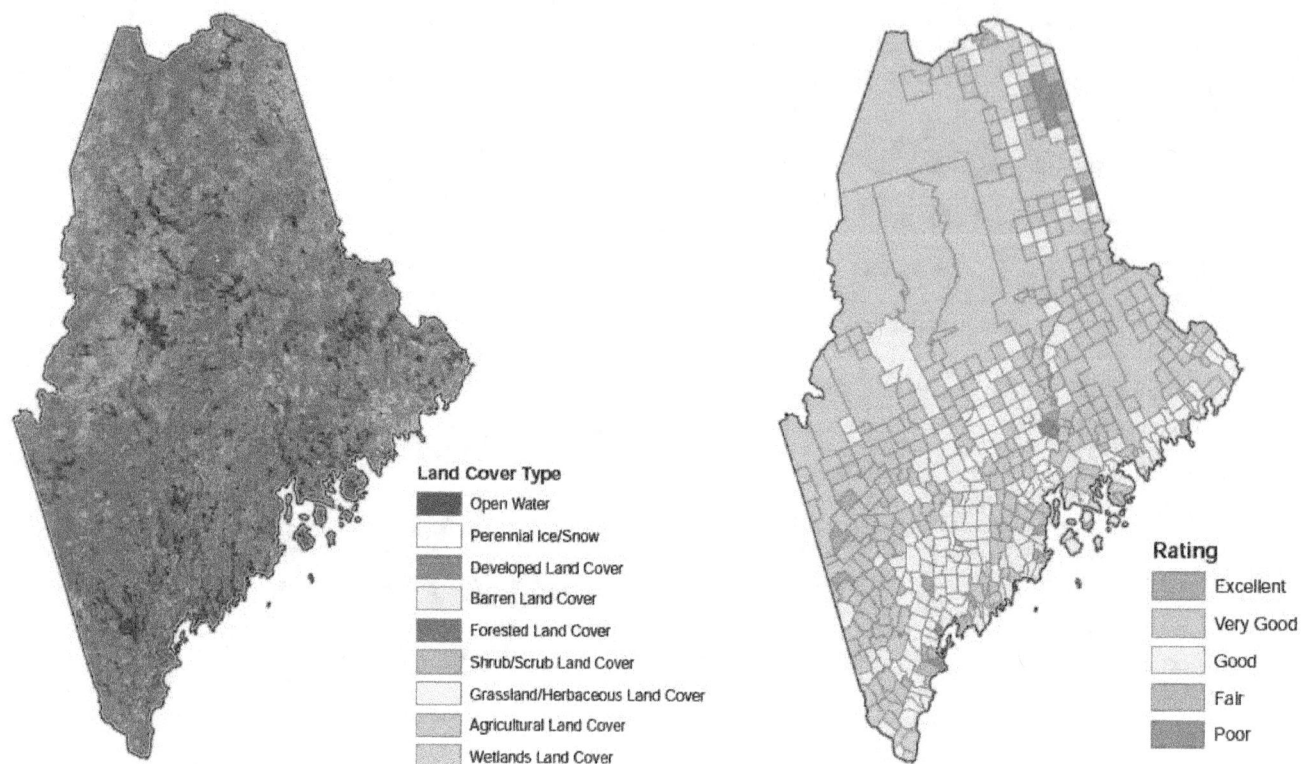

Land Cover Type

■ Open Water
□ Perennial Ice/Snow
▨ Developed Land Cover
░ Barren Land Cover
▨ Forested Land Cover
▨ Shrub/Scrub Land Cover
□ Grassland/Herbaceous Land Cover
▨ Agricultural Land Cover
▨ Wetlands Land Cover

Figure ME-9.—Classified land cover.

Rating

▨ Excellent
▨ Very Good
□ Good
▨ Fair
▨ Poor

Figure ME-10.—Relative comparisons of urban and community forests for county subdivisions.

Classified Land-cover Characteristics

Maine's landcover is dominated by forest land (Fig. ME-9). The characteristics as a percent of the total land area in Maine are (Tables ME-8 through 10):

- Forested—73.5 percent
- Agricultural—12.8 percent
- Scrub/shrub—7.2 percent
- Developed—3.6 percent
- Wetland—1.4 percent
- Grassland—0.8 percent
- Barren—0.6 percent

Relative Comparisons of Urban and Community Forests

Out of the 111 Maine communities, three received a rating of excellent and 14 received a rating of poor (Table ME-12). Of the 531 county subdivisions, seven had a rating of excellent and 13 were rated poor (Fig. ME-10, Table ME-13); and out of 16 counties, two were given a rating of excellent and four were given a rating of poor (Table ME-14). Variability of assessment scores is a product of the difference in land cover distributions and the percentage of canopy cover within the population density classes and mapping zones (Fig ME-10; Tables ME-11 through 14).

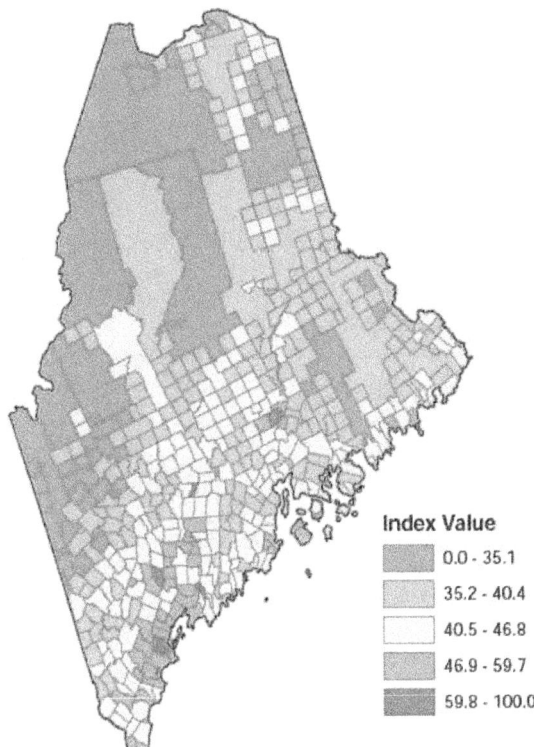

Index Value

- 0.0 - 35.1
- 35.2 - 40.4
- 40.5 - 46.8
- 46.9 - 59.7
- 59.8 - 100.0

Figure ME-11.—Planting priority index for county subdivisions. The higher the index value, the greater priority for planting.

Priority Areas for Tree Planting

Priority areas for planting tend to be highest in more urbanized areas due to higher population density (Fig. ME-11; Tables ME-15 through 17). These index values can also be produced using high resolution cover data to determine local planting priority areas (e.g., neighborhoods).

Urban Tree Benefits

The following forest attributes are estimated for the urban or community land in Maine (Table ME-1). These are rough estimates of values. More localized data are needed for more precise estimates, but these values reveal first-order approximations.

- 74.9 million trees
- 14.3 million metric tons of C stored ($326 million value)
- 471,000 metric tons/year of C sequestered ($10.7 million value)
- 8,670 metric tons/year total pollution removal ($74.1 million value)
  - 135 metric tons/year of CO removed ($189,900 value)
  - 832 metric tons/year NO_2 removed ($8.2 million value)
  - 5,040 metric tons/year of O_3 removed ($49.9 million value)
  - 443 metric tons/year of SO_2 removed ($1.1 million value)
  - 2,217 metric tons/year of PM_{10} removed ($14.7 million value).

Summary

The data presented in this report provide a better understanding of Maine's urban and community forests. This information can be used to advance urban and community forestry policy and management that could improve environmental quality and human health throughout the state.

These data establish a baseline to assess future change and can be used to understand:

- Extent of the urban and community forest resource
- Variations in the resource across the state
- Magnitude and value of the urban and community forest resource
- Urban growth in Maine
- Implications of policy decisions related to urban sprawl and urban and community forest management

MASSACHUSETTS' URBAN AND COMMUNITY FORESTS

Summary

Urban or community land in Massachusetts comprises about 40.4 percent of the state land area in 2000, an increase from 35.9 percent in 1990. Statewide tree canopy cover averages 61.8 percent and tree cover in urban or community areas is about 45.5 percent, with 19.4 percent impervious surface cover and 56.5 percent of the total green space covered by tree canopy cover. Statewide, urban or community land in Massachusetts has an estimated 178 million trees, which store about 34 million metric tons of carbon ($775.2 million), and annually remove about 1.1 million metric tons of carbon ($25.5 million) and 28,850 metric tons of air pollution ($244.7 million) (Table MA-1).

Tables MA-2 through MA-17 are not printed in this report but are available on the CD located on the inside back cover, and at http://www.nrs.fs.fed.us/data/urban.

Table MA-1.—Statewide summary of population, area, population density, tree canopy and impervious surface land cover, and urban tree benefits in urban, community, and urban or community areas.

Massachusetts		Statewide	Urban [a]	Community [b]	Urban or community [c]
Population	2000	6,349,097	5,801,367	4,512,423	n/a
	1990	6,016,425	5,069,603	4,235,869	n/a
	% Change (1990-2000)	5.5	14.4	6.5	n/a
	% Total population (2000)	100.0	91.4	71.1	n/a
Total area	km^2 (2000)	27,336.2	7,475.3	4,848.4	8,611.8
	km^2 (1990)	27,336.2	6,428.2	4,615.8	7,638.1
	% Change (1990-2000)	0.0	16.3	5.0	12.7
Land area	km^2 (2000)	20,308.5	7,230.4	4,563.4	8,205.9
	% Land area (2000)	100.0	35.6	22.5	40.4
	km^2 (1990)	20,308.5	6,256.0	4,355.0	7,295.1
	% Land area (1990)	100.0	30.8	21.4	35.9
	% Change (1990-2000)	0.0	15.6	4.8	12.5
Population density (people/land area km^2)	2000	312.6	802.4	988.8	n/a
	1990	296.3	810.4	972.7	n/a
	% Change (1990-2000)	5.5	-1.0	1.7	n/a
Tree canopy cover (2000)	km^2	12,560.1	3,148.7	1,835.6	3,731.9
	% Land area	61.8	43.5	40.2	45.5
	Per capita (m^2/person)	1,978.2	542.8	406.8	n/a
	% Canopy green space [d]	67.9	55.3	53.4	56.5
Total green space (2000) [e]	km^2	18,502.7	5,694.1	3,434.2	6,610.6
	% Land area	91.1	78.8	75.3	80.6
Available green space (2000) [f]	km^2	5,953.5	2,554.7	1,604.7	2,888.2
	% Land area	29.3	35.3	35.2	35.2
Impervious surface cover (2000)	km^2	1,805.8	1,536.3	1,129.2	1,595.4
	% Land area	8.9	21.2	24.7	19.4
	Per capita (m^2/person)	284.4	264.8	250.2	n/a
	Estimated number of trees	n/a	150,200,000	87,500,000	178,000,000
Urban tree benefits (2000)	**Carbon**				
	Carbon stored (metric tons)	n/a	28,700,000	16,700,000	34,000,000
	Carbon stored ($)	n/a	$654,400,000	$380,800,000	$775,200,000
	Carbon sequestered (metric tons/year)	n/a	945,000	551,000	1,120,000
	Carbon sequestered ($/year)	n/a	$21,546,000	$12,563,000	$25,536,000
	Pollution				
	CO removed (metric tons/year)	n/a	586	342	695
	CO removed ($/year)	n/a	$824,900	$480,900	$977,700
	NO$_2$ removed (metric tons/year)	n/a	3,619	2,110	4,289
	NO$_2$ removed ($/year)	n/a	$35,848,600	$20,898,500	$42,488,700
	O$_3$ removed (metric tons/year)	n/a	13,201	7,696	15,646
	O$_3$ removed ($/year)	n/a	$130,770,000	$76,234,000	$154,992,000
	SO$_2$ removed (metric tons/year)	n/a	1,635	953	1,938
	SO$_2$ removed ($/year)	n/a	$3,965,100	$2,311,500	$4,699,600
	PM$_{10}$ removed (metric tons/year)	n/a	5,304	3,092	6,286
	PM$_{10}$ removed ($/year)	n/a	$35,079,900	$20,450,300	$41,577,600
	Total pollution removal (metric tons/year)	n/a	24,350	14,190	28,850
	Total pollution removal ($/year)	n/a	$206,500,000	$120,400,000	$244,700,000

[a] Urban land is based on population density and was delimited using the U.S. Census definitions of urbanized areas and urban clusters. [b] Community land is based on jurisdictional or political boundaries of communities based on U.S. Census definitions of incorporated or census designated places. [c] Urban or communities is land that is urban, community, or both. Communities may include all, some, or no urban land within their boundaries. [d] Canopy green space is the tree canopy cover divided by total green space. [e] Total green space is total area minus impervious surface cover minus water. [f] Available green space is total green space minus tree canopy cover (if the calculated value is less than 0, then value set at 0).

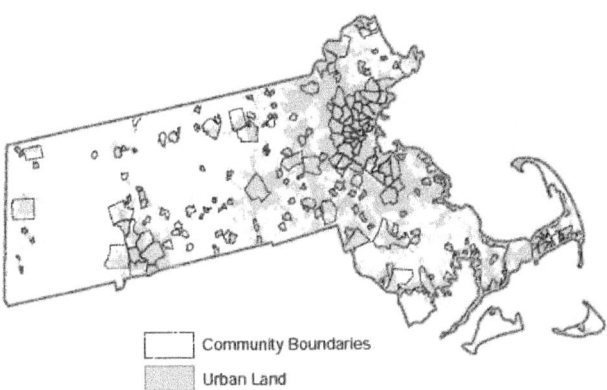

Figure MA-1.—Urban or community land in 2000; urban area relative to community boundaries.

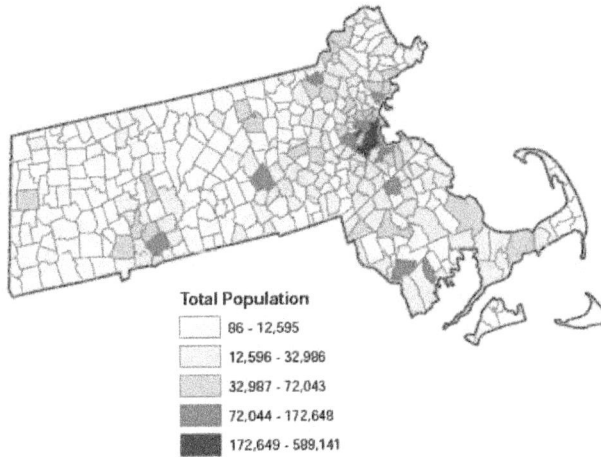

Figure MA-2.—2000 Population within county subdivision boundaries.

Human Population Characteristics and Trends

The population in Massachusetts increased 5.5 percent, from 6,016,425 in 1990 to 6,349,097 in 2000 (Table MA-1). In Massachusetts, 91.4 percent of the state's population is in urban areas (Fig. MA-1), and 71.1 percent of the population is within communities (Fig. MA-2).

Urban and Community Land

Urban land comprises 35.6 percent of the land area of Massachusetts, while lands within communities make up 22.5 percent of the state (Fig. MA-1). Between 1990 and 2000, urban area increased 15.6 percent, while community land increased from 21.4 to 22.5 percent (Table MA-1). Urban area in Massachusetts is projected to increase to 61 percent by 2050, based on average urban growth pattern of the 1990s (Nowak and Walton 2005). Both urban land (attaining minimum population density) and community land (political boundaries) increased from 1990 to 2000. The percentages are calculated using the total (water and land) area of the geopolitical units derived from U.S. Census cartographic boundary data. Percent urban land varied across the state (Fig. MA-3; Tables MA-2 through 4).

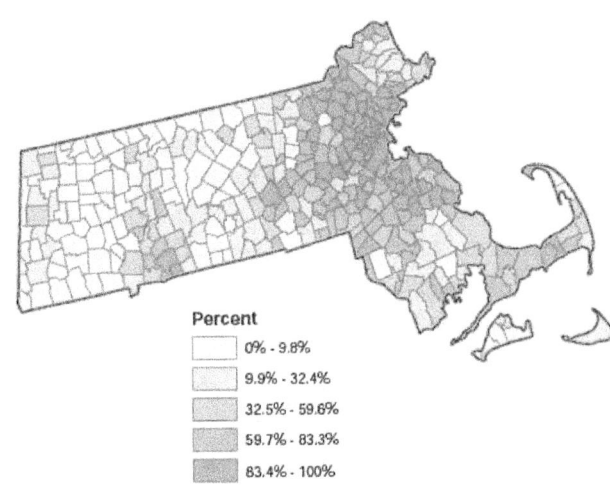

Figure MA-3.—Percent of community subdivision area classified as urban land in 2000.

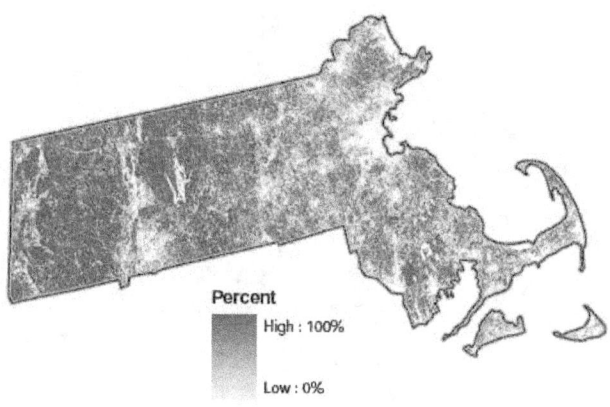

Figure MA-4.—Percentage tree canopy cover.

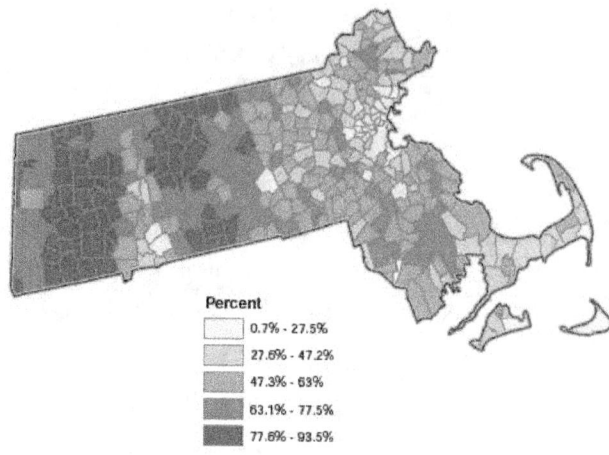

Percent
- 0.7% - 27.5%
- 27.6% - 47.2%
- 47.3% - 63%
- 63.1% - 77.5%
- 77.6% - 93.5%

Figure MA-5.—Percentage tree canopy cover within county subdivisions.

Tree Canopy Cover Characteristics

Tree canopy cover in Massachusetts averages 61.8 percent (Fig. MA-4), with 91.1 percent total green space, 67.9 percent canopy green space, and 1,978.2 m^2 of canopy cover per capita. Average tree cover in urban areas in Massachusetts was 43.5 percent, with 78.8 percent total green space, 55.3 percent canopy green space, and 542.8 m^2 of canopy cover per capita. Within community lands in Massachusetts, average tree cover was 40.2 percent, with 75.3 percent total green space, 53.4 percent canopy green space, and 406.8 m^2 of canopy cover per capita (Table MA-1). Tree canopy cover, canopy green space, and tree cover per capita varied among communities, county subdivisions, and counties (Fig. MA-5 through 6; Tables MA-5 through 7).

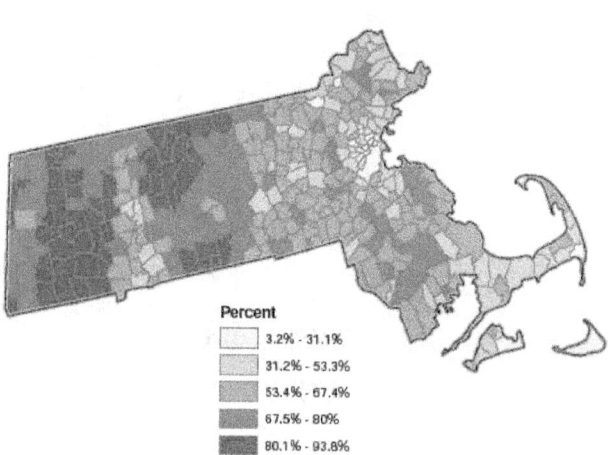

Percent
- 3.2% - 31.1%
- 31.2% - 53.3%
- 53.4% - 67.4%
- 67.5% - 80%
- 80.1% - 93.8%

Figure MA-6.—Percentage tree canopy green space in county subdivisions.

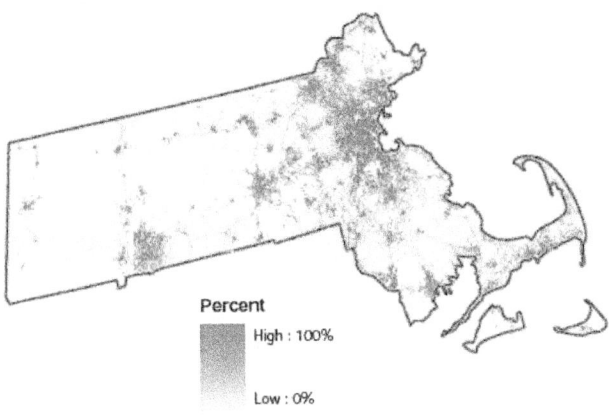

Figure MA-7.—Percentage impervious surface cover.

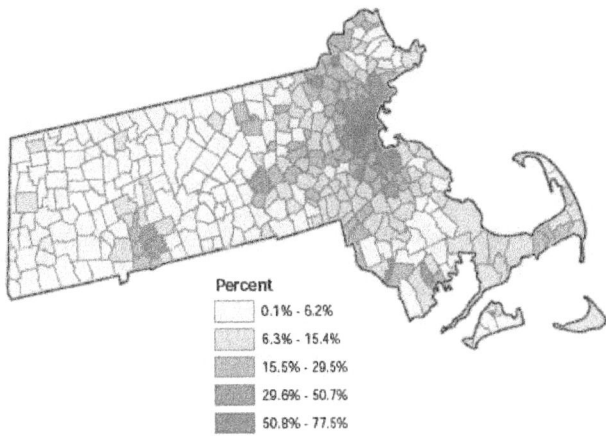

Figure MA-8.—Percentage impervious surface cover within county subdivisions.

Impervious Surface Cover Characteristics

Average impervious surface cover in Massachusetts is 8.9 percent of the land area (Fig. MA-7), with 284.4 m^2 of impervious surface cover per capita. Average impervious surface cover in urban areas was 21.2 percent, with 264.8 m^2 of impervious surface cover per capita. Within community lands in Massachusetts, average impervious surface cover was 24.7 percent with 250.2 m^2 of impervious surface cover per capita (Table MA-1). Impervious surface cover varied across the state (Fig. MA-8; Tables MA-5 through 7).

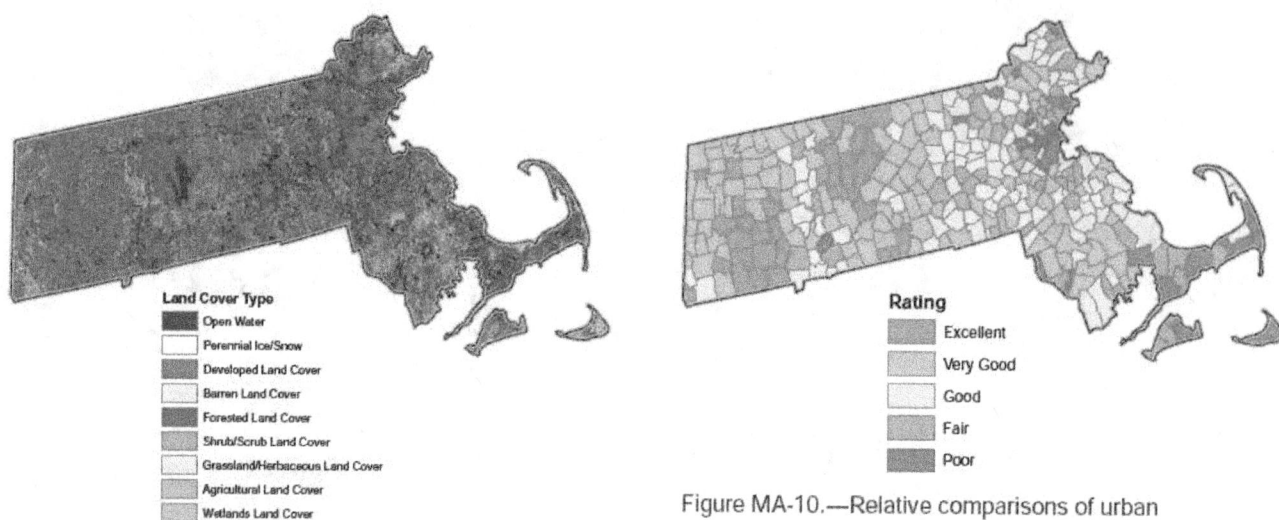

Figure MA-9.—Classified land cover.

Figure MA-10.—Relative comparisons of urban and community forests for county subdivisions.

Classified Land-cover Characteristics

Massachusetts's landcover is dominated by forest land (Fig. MA-9). The characteristics as a percent of the total land area in Massachusetts are (Tables MA-8 through 10):

- Forested—54.6 percent
- Developed—24.4 percent
- Agricultural—16.2 percent
- Wetland—1.9 percent
- Scrub/shrub—1.2 percent
- Barren—1.0 percent
- Grassland—0.6 percent

Relative Comparisons of Urban and Community Forests

Out of the 235 Massachusetts communities, one received a rating of excellent and 47 received a rating of poor (Table MA-12). Of the 351 county subdivisions, 35 had a rating of excellent and 37 were rated poor (Fig. MA-10, Table MA-13); and out of 14 counties, four were given a rating of excellent and three were given a rating of poor (Table MA-14). Variability of assessment scores is a product of the difference in land cover distributions and the percentage of canopy cover within the population density classes and mapping zones (Fig. MA-10; Tables MA-11 through 14).

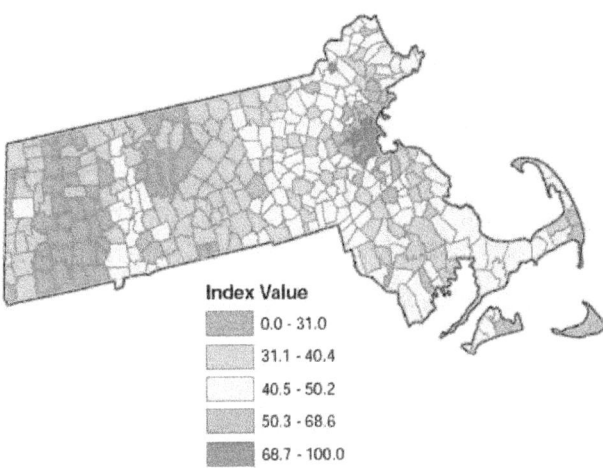

Figure MA-11.—Planting priority index for county subdivisions. The higher the index value, the greater priority for planting.

Index Value
- 0.0 - 31.0
- 31.1 - 40.4
- 40.5 - 50.2
- 50.3 - 68.6
- 68.7 - 100.0

Priority Areas for Tree Planting

Priority areas for planting tend to be highest in more urbanized areas due to higher population density (Fig. MA-11; Tables MA-15 through 17). These index values can also be produced using high resolution cover data to determine local planting priority areas (e.g. neighborhoods).

Urban Tree Benefits

The following forest attributes are estimated for the urban or community land in Massachusetts (Table MA-1). These are rough estimates of values. More localized data are needed for more precise estimates, but these values reveal first-order approximations.

- 178 million trees
- 34 million metric tons of C stored ($775.2 million value)
- 1.1 million metric tons/year of C sequestered ($25.5 million value)
- 28,850 metric tons/year total pollution removal ($244.7 million value)
  - 695 metric tons/year of CO removed ($977,700 value)
  - 4,289 metric tons/year NO_2 removed ($42.5 million value)
  - 15,646 metric tons/year of O_3 removed ($155 million value)
  - 1,938 metric tons/year of SO_2 removed ($4.7 million value)
  - 6,286 metric tons/year of PM_{10} removed ($41.6 million value).

Summary

The data presented in this report provide a better understanding of Massachusetts's urban and community forests. This information can be used to advance urban and community forestry policy and management that could improve environmental quality and human health throughout the state.

These data establish a baseline to assess future change and can be used to understand:

- Extent of the urban and community forest resource
- Variations in the resource across the state
- Magnitude and value of the urban and community forest resource
- Urban growth in Massachusetts
- Implications of policy decisions related to urban sprawl and urban and community forest management

NE   HAM SHIRE'S URBAN AND COMMUNITY FORESTS

Summary

Urban or community land in New Hampshire comprises about 10.3 percent of the state land area in 2000, an increase from 9.0 percent in 1990. Statewide tree canopy cover averages 75.3 percent and tree cover in urban or community areas is about 53.8 percent, with 11.8 percent impervious surface cover and 60.9 percent of the total green space covered by tree canopy cover. Statewide, urban or community land in New Hampshire has an estimated 61.4 million trees, which store about 11.7 million metric tons of carbon ($266.8 million), and annually remove about 387,000 metric tons of carbon ($8.8 million) and 6,390 metric tons of air pollution ($55 million) (Table NH-1).

Tables NH-2 through NH-17 are not printed in this report but are available on the CD located on the inside back cover and at http://www.nrs.fs.fed.us/data/urban.

Table NH-1.—Statewide summary of population, area, population density, tree canopy and impervious surface land cover, and urban tree benefits in urban, community, and urban or community areas.

New ampshire		Statewide	Urban [a]	Community [b]	Urban or community [c]
Population	2000	1,235,786	732,335	586,440	n/a
	1990	1,109,252	565,670	547,324	n/a
	% Change (1990-2000)	11.4	29.5	7.1	n/a
	% Total population (2000)	100.0	59.3	47.5	n/a
Total area	km² (2000)	24,216.2	1,487.7	1,714.8	2,480.7
	km² (1990)	24,216.2	1,102.9	1,703.1	2,163.9
	% Change (1990-2000)	0.0	34.9	0.7	14.6
Land area	km² (2000)	23,264.5	1,448.6	1,654.9	2,396.9
	% Land area (2000)	100.0	6.2	7.1	10.3
	km² (1990)	23,264.5	1,088.8	1,643.6	2,096.9
	% Land area (1990)	100.0	4.7	7.1	9.0
	% Change (1990-2000)	0.0	33.0	0.7	14.3
Population density (people/land area km²)	2000	53.1	505.6	354.4	n/a
	1990	47.7	519.5	333.0	n/a
	% Change (1990-2000)	11.4	-2.7	6.4	n/a
Tree canopy cover (2000)	km²	17,528.6	640.0	916.6	1,288.4
	% Land area	75.3	44.2	55.4	53.8
	Per capita (m²/person)	14,184.2	874.0	1,563.0	n/a
	% Canopy green space [d]	76.9	53.3	63.0	60.9
Total green space (2000) [e]	km²	22,800.3	1,201.6	1,455.1	2,113.9
	% Land area	98.0	83.0	87.9	88.2
Available green space (2000) [f]	km²	5,272.8	562.1	539.0	826.2
	% Land area	22.7	38.8	32.6	34.5
Impervious surface cover (2000)	km²	464.2	247.0	199.8	282.9
	% Land area	2.0	17.0	12.1	11.8
	Per capita (m²/person)	375.6	337.2	340.6	n/a
	Estimated number of trees	n/a	30,500,000	43,700,000	61,400,000
	Carbon				
	Carbon stored (metric tons)	n/a	5,800,000	8,300,000	11,700,000
	Carbon stored ($)	n/a	$132,200,000	$189,200,000	$266,800,000
	Carbon sequestered (metric tons/year)	n/a	192,000	275,000	387,000
	Carbon sequestered ($/year)	n/a	$4,378,000	$6,270,000	$8,824,000
	Pollution				
Urban tree benefits (2000)	CO removed (metric tons/year)	n/a	56	80	113
	CO removed ($/year)	n/a	$79,100	$113,300	$159,200
	NO₂ removed (metric tons/year)	n/a	348	498	700
	NO₂ removed ($/year)	n/a	$3,444,500	$4,933,000	$6,933,800
	O₃ removed (metric tons/year)	n/a	1,868	2,676	3,761
	O₃ removed ($/year)	n/a	$18,507,000	$26,505,000	$37,256,000
	SO₂ removed (metric tons/year)	n/a	162	231	325
	SO₂ removed ($/year)	n/a	$391,900	$561,300	$788,900
	PM₁₀ removed (metric tons/year	n/a	742	1,063	1,495
	PM₁₀ removed ($/year)	n/a	$4,910,500	$7,032,500	$9,884,900
	Total pollution removal (metric tons/year)	n/a	3,180	4,550	6,390
	Total pollution removal ($/year)	n/a	$27,300,000	$39,100,000	$55,000,000

[a] Urban land is based on population density and was delimited using the U.S. Census defini ions of urbanized areas and urban clusters. [b] Community land is based on jurisdictional or political boundaries of communities based on U.S. Census defini ions of incorporated or census designated places. [c] Urban or communities is land that is urban, community, or both. Communities may include all, some, or no urban land within their boundaries. [d] Canopy green space is the tree canopy cover divided by total green space. [e] Total green space is total area minus impervious surface cover minus water. [f] Available green space is total green space minus tree canopy cover (if the calculated value is less than 0, then value set at 0).

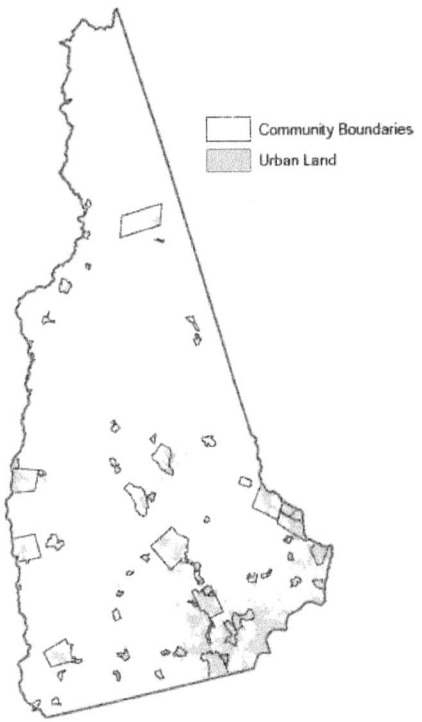

Figure NH-1.—Urban or community land in 2000; urban area relative to community boundaries.

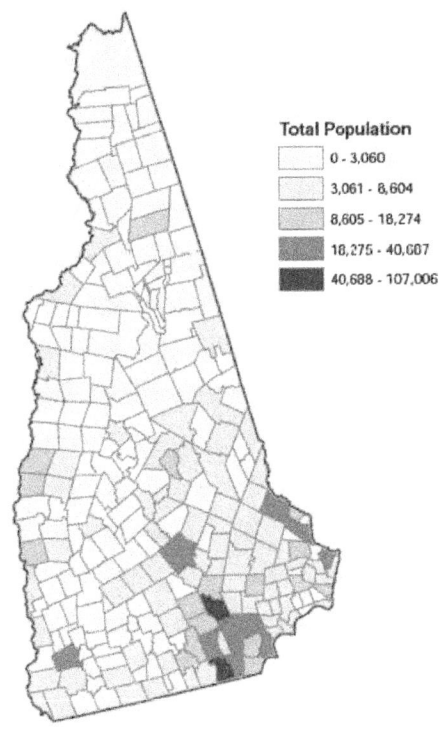

Figure NH-2.—2000 Population within county subdivision boundaries.

Human Population Characteristics and Trends

The population in New Hampshire increased 11.4 percent, from 1,109,252 in 1990 to 1,235,786 in 2000 (Table NH-1). In New Hampshire, 59.3 percent of the state's population is in urban areas (Fig. NH-1), and 47.5 percent of the population is within communities (Fig. NH-2).

Urban and Community Land

Urban land comprises 6.2 percent of the land area of New Hampshire, while lands within communities make up 7.1 percent of the state (Fig. NH-1). Between 1990 and 2000, urban area increased 33 percent, while community land increased slightly (Table NH-1). Urban area in New Hampshire is projected to increase to 17.1 percent by 2050, based on average urban growth pattern of the 1990s (Nowak and Walton 2005). Both urban land (attaining minimum population density) and community land (political boundaries) increased from 1990 to 2000. The percentages are calculated using the total (water and land) area of the geopolitical units derived from U.S. Census cartographic boundary data. Percent urban land varied across the state (Fig. NH-3; Tables NH-2 through 4).

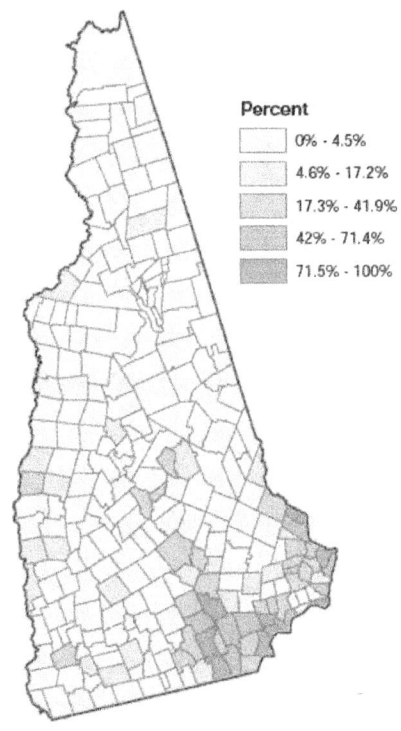

Figure NH-3.—Percent of community subdivision area classified as urban land in 2000.

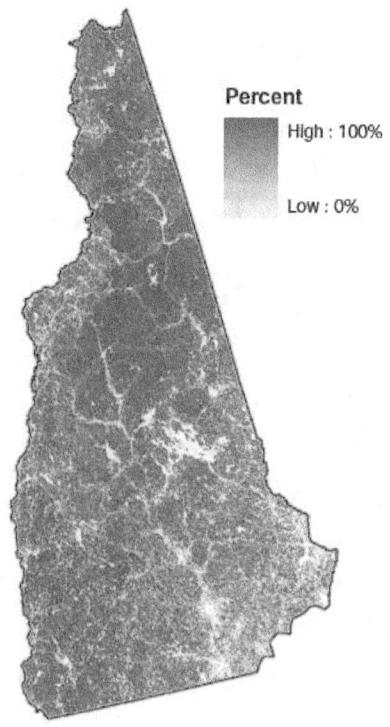

Figure NH-4.—Percentage tree
canopy cover.

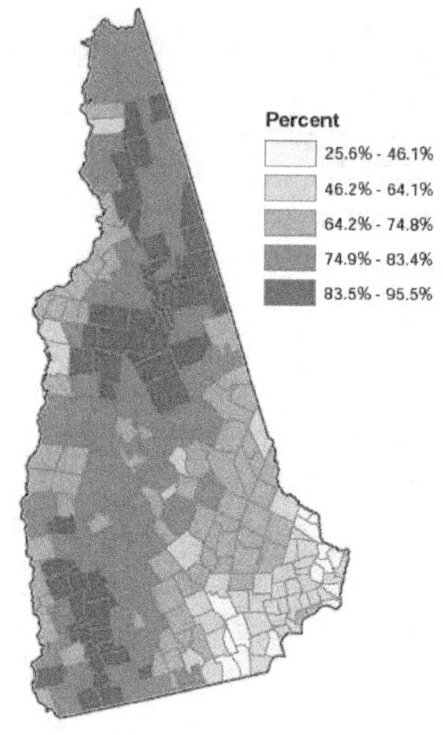

Percent
	25.6% - 46.1%
	46.2% - 64.1%
	64.2% - 74.8%
	74.9% - 83.4%
	83.5% - 95.5%

Figure NH-5.—Percentage tree canopy
cover within county subdivisions.

Tree Canopy Cover Characteristics

Tree canopy cover in New Hampshire averages 75.3 percent (Fig. NH-4), with
98 percent total green space, 76.9 percent canopy green space, and 14,184.2 m^2
of canopy cover per capita. Average tree cover in urban areas in New Hampshire
was 44.2 percent, with 83.0 percent total green space, 55.3 percent canopy
green space, and 874 m^2 of canopy cover per capita. Within community lands
in New Hampshire, average tree cover was 55.4 percent, with 87.9 percent total
green space, 63.0 percent canopy green space, and 1,563 m^2 of canopy cover per
capita (Table NH-1). Tree canopy cover, canopy green space, and tree cover per
capita varied among communities, county subdivisions, and counties (Fig. NH-5
through 6; Tables NH-5 through 7).

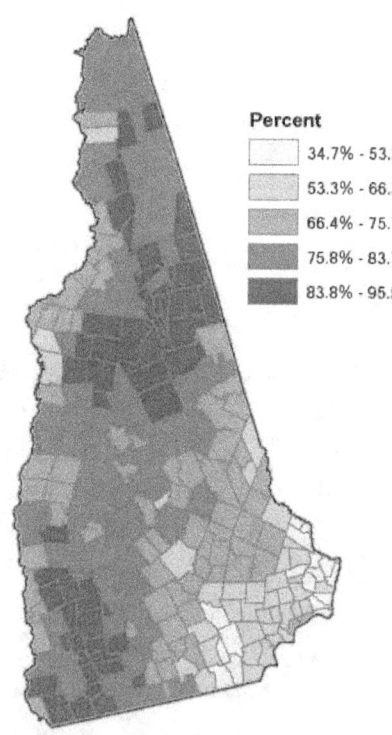

Percent
	34.7% - 53.2%
	53.3% - 66.3%
	66.4% - 75.7%
	75.8% - 83.7%
	83.8% - 95.5%

Figure NH-6.—Percentage tree
canopy green space in county
subdivisions.

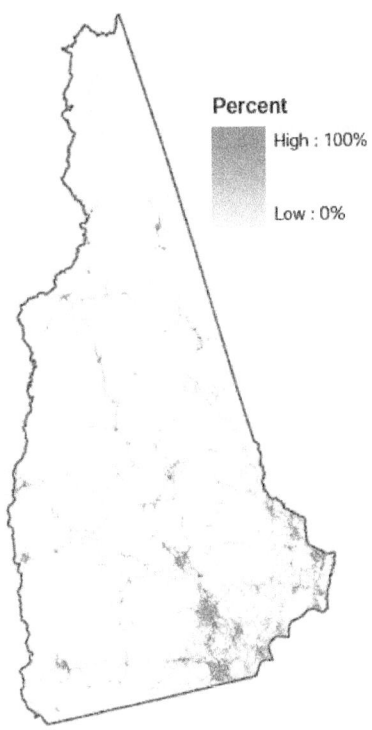

Figure NH-7.—Percentage
impervious surface cover.

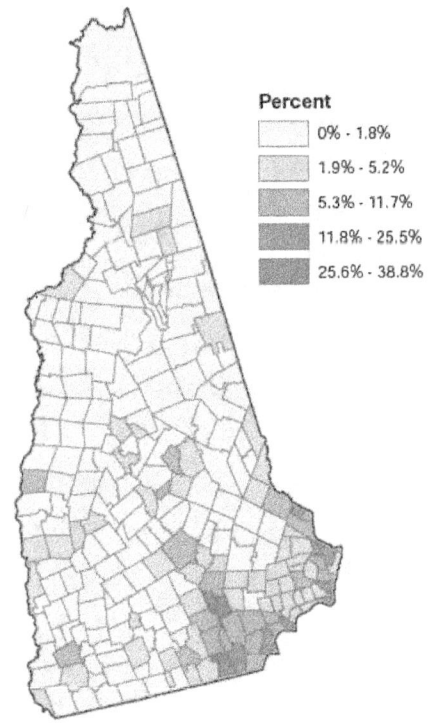

Figure NH-8.—Percentage
impervious surface cover within
county subdivisions.

Impervious Surface Cover Characteristics

Average impervious surface cover in New Hampshire is 2 percent of the land area
(Fig. NH-7), with 375.6 m^2 of impervious surface cover per capita. Average impervious
surface cover in urban areas was 17 percent, with 337.2 m^2 of impervious surface cover
per capita. Within community lands in New Hampshire, average impervious surface cover
was 12.1 percent with 340.6 m^2 of impervious surface cover per capita (Table NH-1).
Impervious surface cover varied across the state (Fig. NH-8; Tables NH-5 through 7).

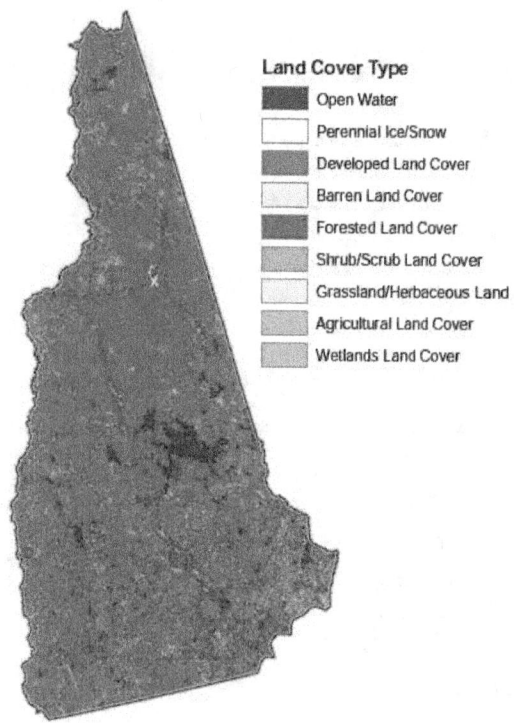

Figure NH-9.—Classified land cover.

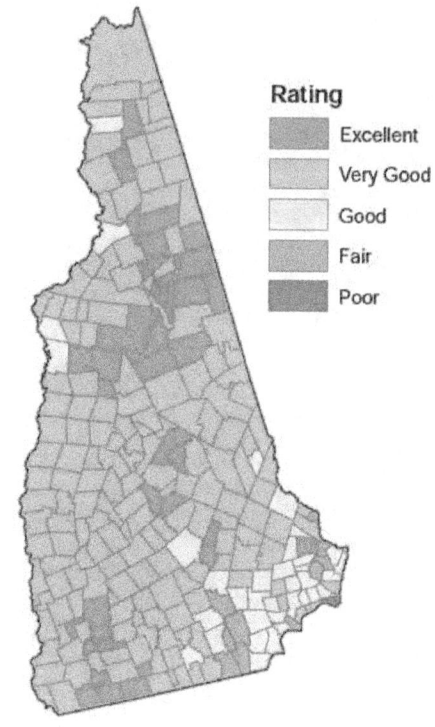

Figure NH-10.—Relative comparisons of urban and community forests for county subdivisions.

Classified Land-cover Characteristics

New Hampshire's landcover is dominated by forest land (Fig. NH-9). The characteristics as a percent of the total land area in New Hampshire are (Tables NH-8 through 10):

- Forested—80.6 percent
- Agricultural—8.4 percent
- Developed—7.8 percent
- Scrub/shrub—2.0 percent
- Wetland—0.7 percent
- Barren—0.4 percent
- Grassland—0.3 percent

Relative Comparisons of Urban and Community Forests

Out of the 60 New Hampshire communities, five received a rating of excellent and two received a rating of poor (Table NH-12). Of the 259 county subdivisions, 42 had a rating of excellent and one was rated poor (Fig. NH-10, Table NH-13); and out of 10 counties, seven were given a rating of excellent and one was given a rating of poor (Table NH-14). Variability of assessment scores is a product of the difference in land cover distributions and the percentage of canopy cover within the population density classes and mapping zones (Fig. NH-10; Tables NH-11 through 14).

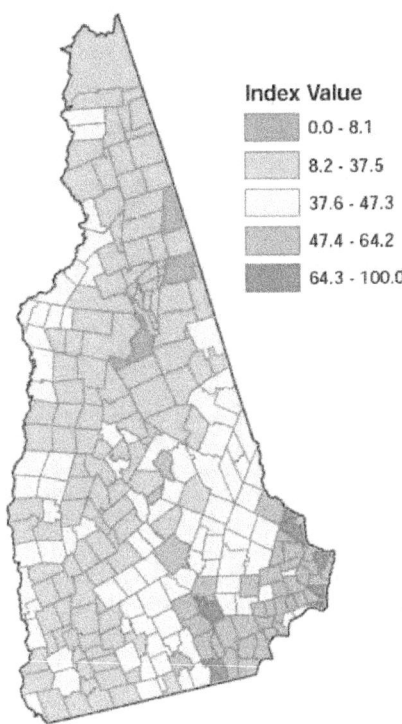

Index Value

- 0.0 - 8.1
- 8.2 - 37.5
- 37.6 - 47.3
- 47.4 - 64.2
- 64.3 - 100.0

Figure NH-11.—Planting priority index for county subdivisions. The higher the index value, the greater priority for planting.

Priority Areas for Tree Planting

Priority areas for planting tend to be highest in more urbanized areas due to higher population density (Fig. NH-11; Tables NH-15 through 17). These index values can also be produced using high resolution cover data to determine local planting priority areas (e.g., neighborhoods).

Urban Tree Benefits

The following forest attributes are estimated for the urban or community land in New Hampshire (Table NH-1). These are rough estimates of values. More localized data are needed for more precise estimates, but these values reveal first-order approximations.

- 61.4 million trees
- 11.7 million metric tons of C stored ($266.8 million value)
- 387,000 metric tons/year of C sequestered ($8.8 million value)
- 6,390 metric tons/year total pollution removal ($55 million value)
  - 113 metric tons/year of CO removed ($159,200 value)
  - 700 metric tons/year NO_2 removed ($6.9 million value)
  - 3,761 metric tons/year of O_3 removed ($37.3 million value)
  - 325 metric tons/year of SO_2 removed ($788,900 value)
  - 1,495 metric tons/year of PM_{10} removed ($9.9 million value).

Summary

The data presented in this report provide a better understanding of New Hampshire's urban and community forests. This information can be used to advance urban and community forestry policy and management that could improve environmental quality and human health throughout the state.

These data establish a baseline to assess future change and can be used to understand:

- Extent of the urban and community forest resource
- Variations in the resource across the state
- Magnitude and value of the urban and community forest resource
- Urban growth in New Hampshire
- Implications of policy decisions related to urban sprawl and urban and community forest management

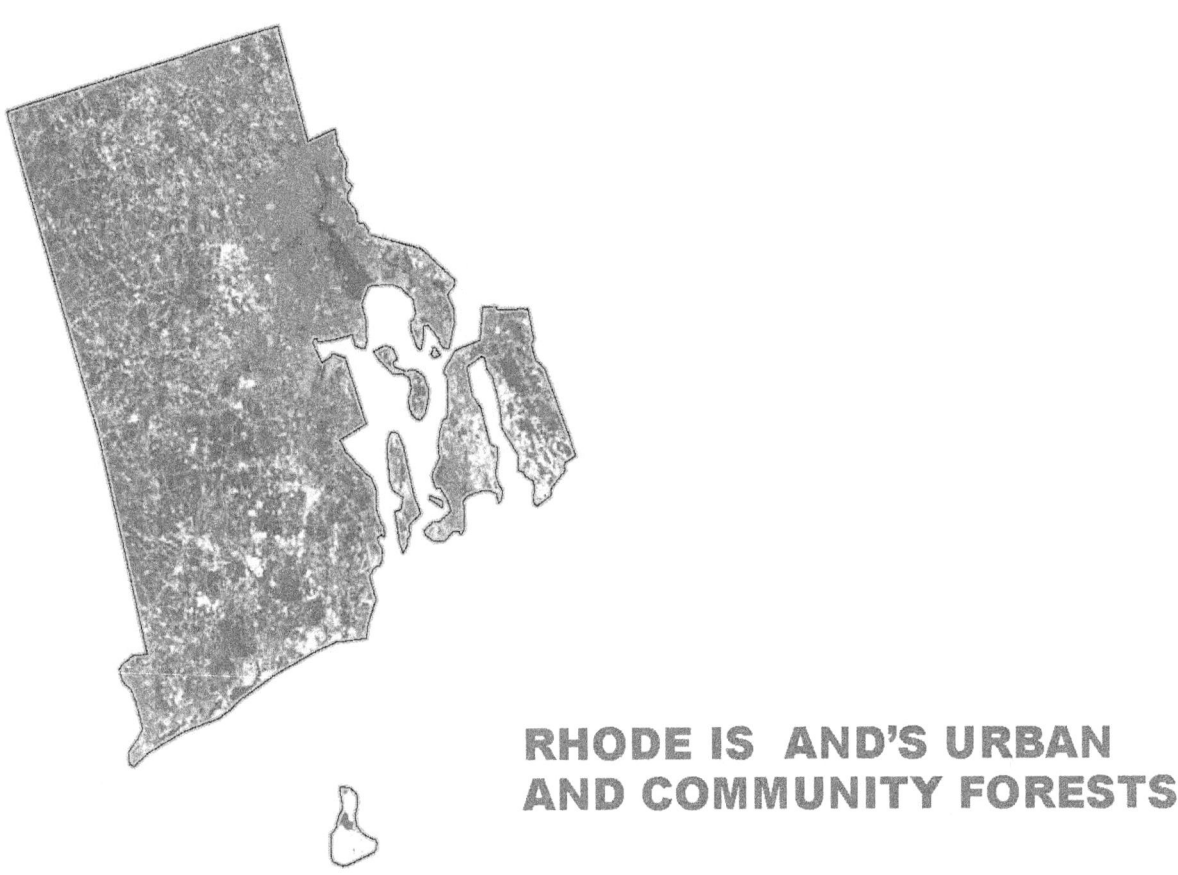

RHODE IS AND'S URBAN AND COMMUNITY FORESTS

Summary

Urban or community land in Rhode Island comprises about 39.4 percent of the state land area in 2000, an increase from 34.3 percent in 1990. Statewide tree canopy cover averages 54.3 percent and tree cover in urban or community areas is about 34.5 percent, with 28.8 percent impervious surface cover and 48.4 percent of the total green space covered by tree canopy cover. Statewide, urban or community land in Rhode Island has an estimated 17.5 million trees, which store about 3.3 million metric tons of carbon ($75.2 million), and annually remove about 110,000 metric tons of carbon ($2.5 million) and 2,660 metric tons of air pollution ($21.6 million) (Table RI-1).

Tables RI-2 through RI-17 are not printed in this report but are available on the CD located on the inside back cover, and at http://www.nrs.fs.fed.us/data/urban.

Table RI-1.—Statewide summary of population, area, population density, tree canopy and impervious surface land cover, and urban tree benefits in urban, community, and urban or community areas.

Rhode Island		Statewide	Urban [a]	Community [b]	Urban or community [c]
Population	2000	1,048,319	953,146	745,534	n/a
	1990	1,003,464	863,381	727,569	n/a
	% Change (1990-2000)	4.5	10.4	2.5	n/a
	% Total population (2000)	100.0	90.9	71.1	n/a
Total area	km² (2000)	4,001.7	1,035.0	608.9	1,126.9
	km² (1990)	4,001.7	866.1	600.9	979.6
	% Change (1990-2000)	0.0	19.5	1.3	15.0
Land area	km² (2000)	2,705.2	996.6	560.4	1,065.5
	% Land area (2000)	100.0	36.8	20.7	39.4
	km² (1990)	2,705.2	848.1	556.8	927.4
	% Land area (1990)	100.0	31.4	20.6	34.3
	% Change (1990-2000)	0.0	17.5	0.7	14.9
Population density (people/land area km²)	2000	387.5	956.4	1,330.3	n/a
	1990	370.9	1,018.0	1,306.7	n/a
	% Change (1990-2000)	4.5	-6.0	1.8	n/a
Tree canopy cover (2000)	km²	1,467.8	333.6	147.4	367.2
	% Land area	54.3	33.5	26.3	34.5
	Per capita (m²/person)	1,400.2	350.0	197.7	n/a
	% Canopy green space [d]	62.3	48.0	42.6	48.4
Total green space (2000) [e]	km²	2,356.7	694.7	346.0	759.0
	% Land area	87.1	69.7	61.7	71.2
Available green space (2000) [f]	km²	890.6	362.5	199.4	393.2
	% Land area	32.9	36.4	35.6	36.9
Impervious surface cover (2000)	km²	348.5	301.9	214.5	306.5
	% Land area	12.9	30.3	38.3	28.8
	Per capita (m²/person)	332.4	316.7	287.6	n/a
Urban tree benefits (2000)	Estimated number of trees	n/a	15,900,000	7,000,000	17,500,000
	Carbon				
	Carbon stored (metric tons)	n/a	3,000,000	1,300,000	3,300,000
	Carbon stored ($)	n/a	$68,400,000	$29,600,000	$75,200,000
	Carbon sequestered (metric tons/year)	n/a	100,000	44,000	110,000
	Carbon sequestered ($/year)	n/a	$2,280,000	$1,003,000	$2,508,000
	Pollution				
	CO removed (metric tons/year)	n/a	40	18	44
	CO removed ($/year)	n/a	$56,200	$24,800	$61,900
	NO₂ removed (metric tons/year)	n/a	319	141	351
	NO₂ removed ($/year)	n/a	$3,161,000	$1,396,300	$3,479,800
	O₃ removed (metric tons/year)	n/a	1,088	481	1,198
	O₃ removed ($/year)	n/a	$10,778,000	$4,761,000	$11,864,000
	SO₂ removed (metric tons/year)	n/a	191	84	210
	SO₂ removed ($/year)	n/a	$462,900	$204,500	$509,500
	PM₁₀ removed (metric tons/year)	n/a	779	344	857
	PM₁₀ removed ($/year)	n/a	$5,149,900	$2,274,900	$5,669,300
	Total pollution removal (metric tons/year)	n/a	2,420	1,070	2,660
	Total pollution removal ($/year)	n/a	$19,600,000	$8,700,000	$21,600,000

[a] Urban land is based on population density and was delimited using the U.S. Census definitions of urbanized areas and urban clusters. [b] Community land is based on jurisdictional or political boundaries of communities based on U.S. Census definitions of incorporated or census designated places. [c] Urban or communities is land that is urban, community, or both. Communities may include all, some, or no urban land within their boundaries. [d] Canopy green space is the tree canopy cover divided by total green space. [e] Total green space is total area minus impervious surface cover minus water. [f] Available green space is total green space minus tree canopy cover (if the calculated value is less than 0, then value set at 0).

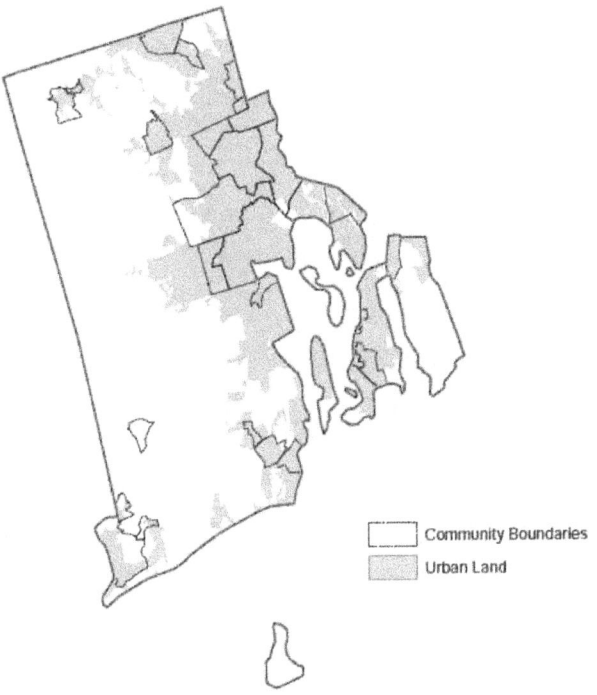

Community Boundaries
Urban Land

Figure RI-1.—Urban or community land
in 2000; urban area relative to community
boundaries.

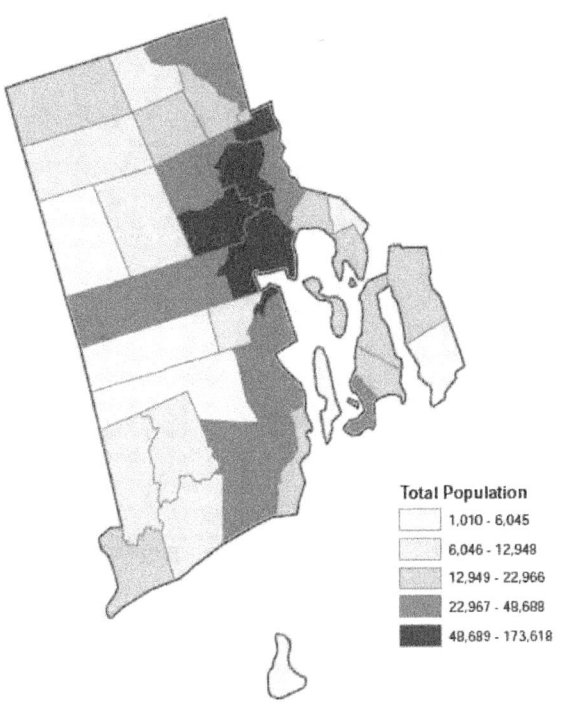

Total Population
1,010 - 6,045
6,046 - 12,948
12,949 - 22,966
22,967 - 49,688
48,689 - 173,618

Figure RI-2.—2000 Population within county
subdivision boundaries.

Human Population Characteristics and Trends

The population in Rhode Island increased 4.5 percent, from 1,003,464 in
1990 to 1,048,319 in 2000 (Table RI-1). In Rhode Island, 90.9 percent of
the state's population is in urban areas (Fig. RI-1), and 71.1 percent of the
population is within communities (Fig. RI-2).

Urban and Community Land

Urban land comprises 36.8 percent of the land area of Rhode Island, while
lands within communities make up 20.7 percent of the state (Fig. RI-1).
Between 1990 and 2000, urban area increased 17.5 percent, while
community land increased slightly (Table RI-1). Urban area in Rhode Island
is projected to increase to 70.5 percent by 2050, based on average urban
growth pattern of the 1990s (Nowak and Walton 2005). Both urban land
(attaining minimum population density) and community land (political
boundaries) increased from 1990 to 2000. The percentages are calculated
using the total (water and land) area of the geopolitical units derived from
U.S. Census cartographic boundary data. Percent urban land varied across
the state (Fig. RI-3; Tables RI-2 through 4).

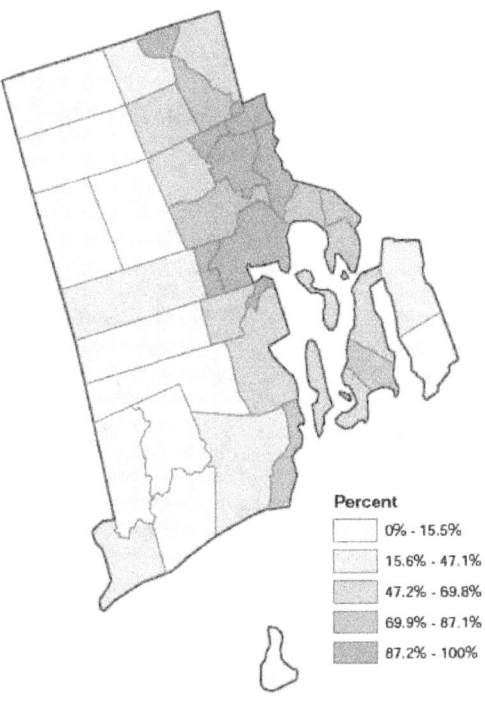

Percent
0% - 15.5%
15.6% - 47.1%
47.2% - 69.8%
69.9% - 87.1%
87.2% - 100%

Figure RI-3.—Percent of community
subdivision area classified as urban land in
2000.

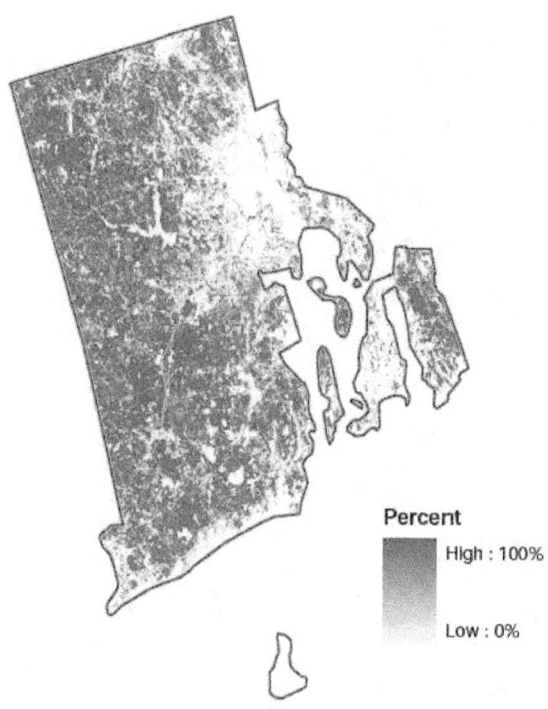

Percent

High : 100%

Low : 0%

Figure RI-4.—Percentage tree canopy cover.

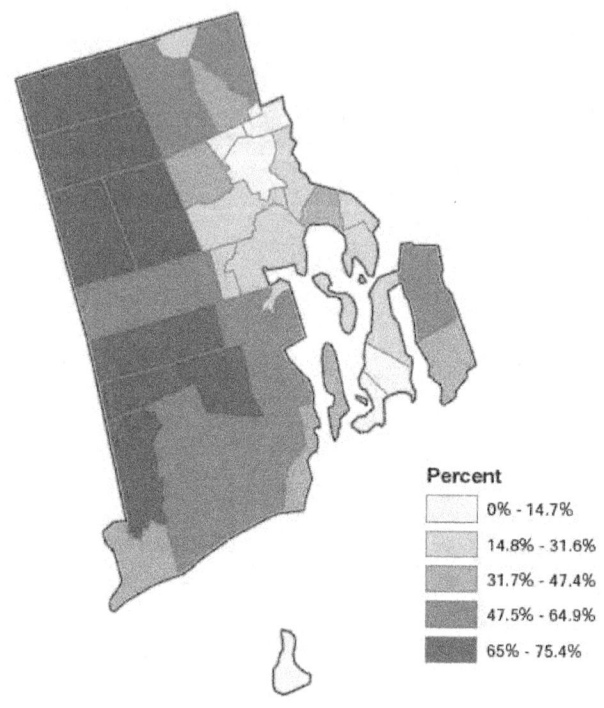

Percent

	0% - 14.7%
	14.8% - 31.6%
	31.7% - 47.4%
	47.5% - 64.9%
	65% - 75.4%

Figure RI-5.—Percentage tree canopy cover within county subdivisions.

Tree Canopy Cover Characteristics

Tree canopy cover in Rhode Island averages 54.3 percent (Fig. RI-4), with 87.1 percent total green space, 62.3 percent canopy green space, and 1,400.2 m^2 of canopy cover per capita. Average tree cover in urban areas in Rhode Island was 33.5 percent, with 69.7 percent total green space, 48 percent canopy green space, and 350 m^2 of canopy cover per capita. Within community lands in Rhode Island, average tree cover was 26.3 percent, with 61.7 percent total green space, 42.6 percent canopy green space, and 197.7 m^2 of canopy cover per capita (Table RI-1). Tree canopy cover, canopy green space, and tree cover per capita varied among communities, county subdivisions, and counties (Fig. RI-5 through 6; Tables RI-5-7).

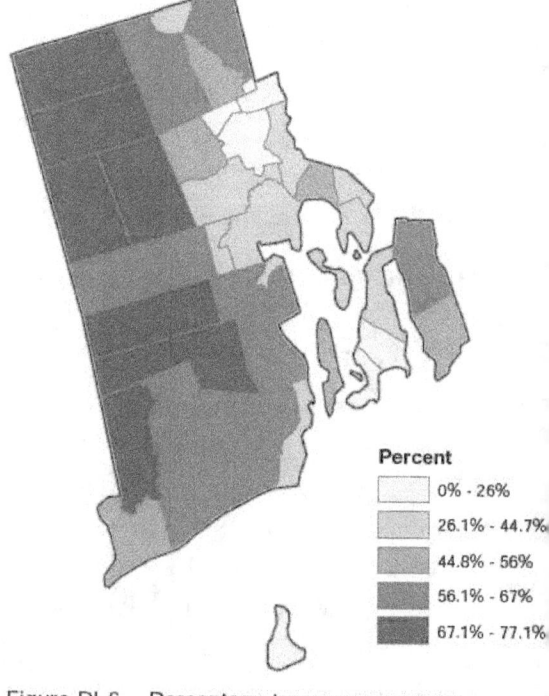

Percent

	0% - 26%
	26.1% - 44.7%
	44.8% - 56%
	56.1% - 67%
	67.1% - 77.1%

Figure RI-6.—Percentage tree canopy green space in county subdivisions.

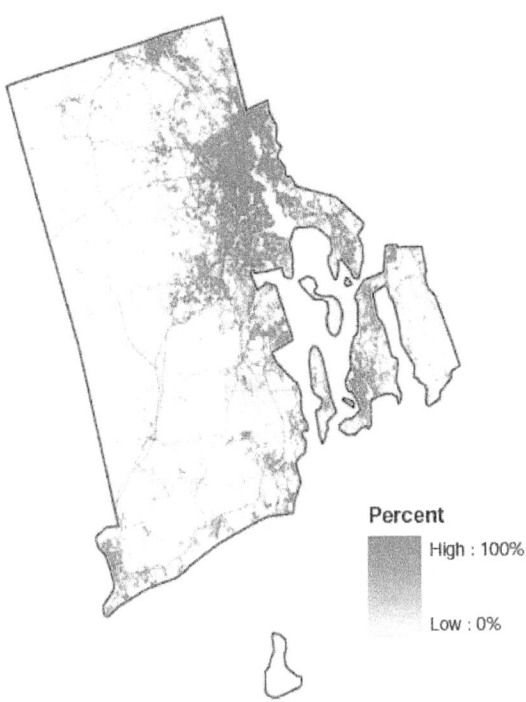

Percent

High : 100%

Low : 0%

Figure RI-7.—Percentage impervious surface cover.

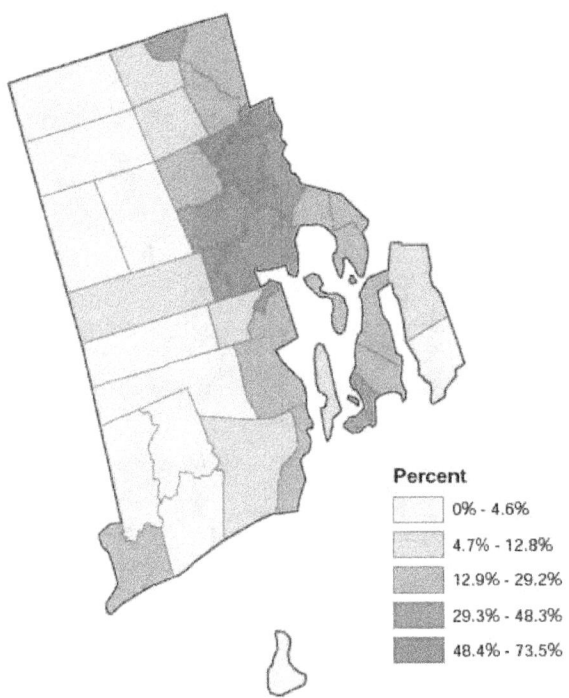

Percent

0% - 4.6%

4.7% - 12.8%

12.9% - 29.2%

29.3% - 48.3%

48.4% - 73.5%

Figure RI-8.—Percentage impervious surface cover within county subdivisions.

Impervious Surface Cover Characteristics

Average impervious surface cover in Rhode Island is 12.9 percent of the land area (Fig. RI-7), with 332.4 m^2 of impervious surface cover per capita. Average impervious surface cover in urban areas was 30.3 percent, with 316.7 m^2 of impervious surface cover per capita. Within community lands in Rhode Island, average impervious surface cover was 38.3 percent with 287.6 m^2 of impervious surface cover per capita (Table RI-1). Impervious surface cover varied across the state (Fig. RI-8; Tables RI-5 through 7).

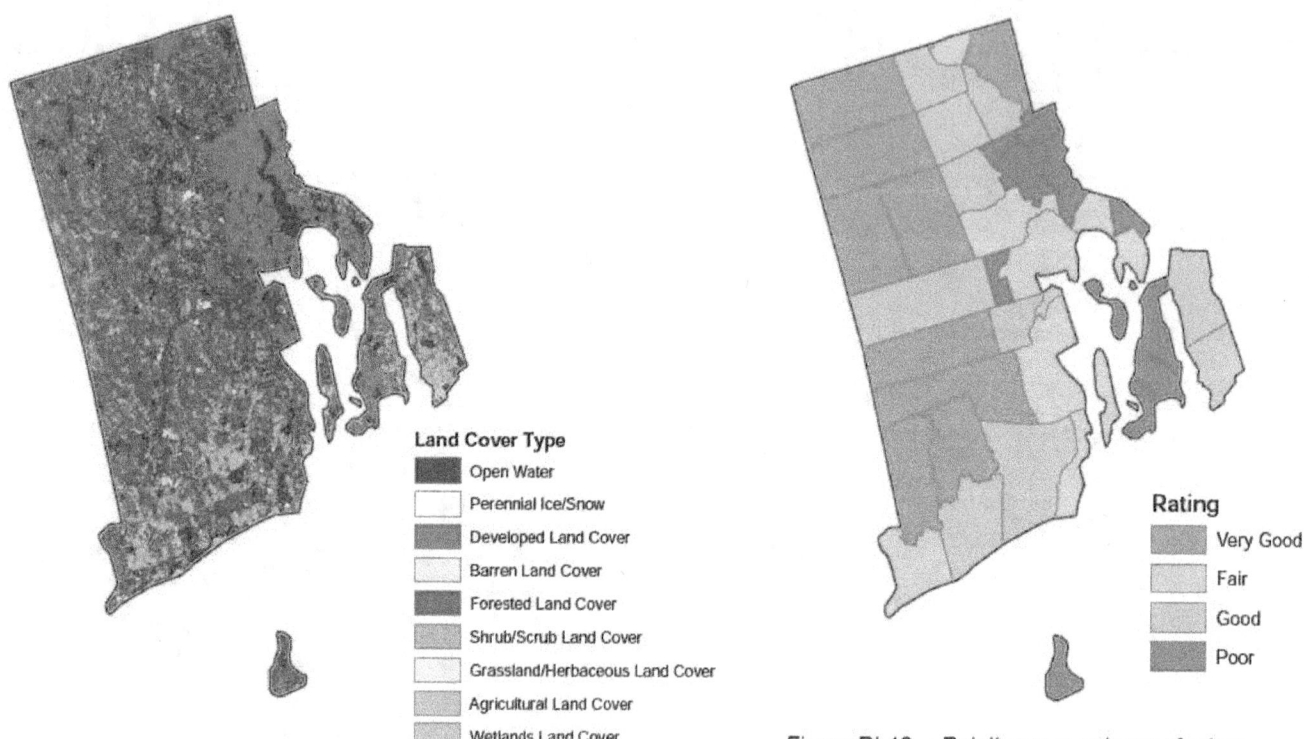

Land Cover Type

Open Water

Perennial Ice/Snow

Developed Land Cover

Barren Land Cover

Forested Land Cover

Shrub/Scrub Land Cover

Grassland/Herbaceous Land Cover

Agricultural Land Cover

Wetlands Land Cover

Figure RI-9.—Classified land cover.

Rating

Very Good

Fair

Good

Poor

Figure RI-10.—Relative comparisons of urban and community forests for county subdivisions.

Classified Land-cover Characteristics

Rhode Island's landcover is dominated by forest land (Fig. RI-9). The characteristics as a percent of the total land area in Rhode Island are (Tables RI-8 through 10):

- Forested—48.1 percent
- Developed—29.6 percent
- Agricultural—17.5 percent
- Wetland—2.0 percent
- Grassland—1.1 percent
- Barren—0.9 percent
- Scrub/shrub—0.8 percent

Relative Comparisons of Urban and Community Forests

Out of the 27 Rhode Island communities, none received a rating of excellent and 10 received a rating of poor (Table RI-12). Of the 39 county subdivisions, none had a rating of excellent and 11 were rated poor (Fig. RI -10, Table RI -13); and out of five counties, one was given a rating of excellent and three were given a rating of poor (Table RI -14). Variability of assessment scores is a product of the difference in land cover distributions and the percentage of canopy cover within the population density classes and mapping zones (Fig. RI-10; Tables RI-11 through 14).

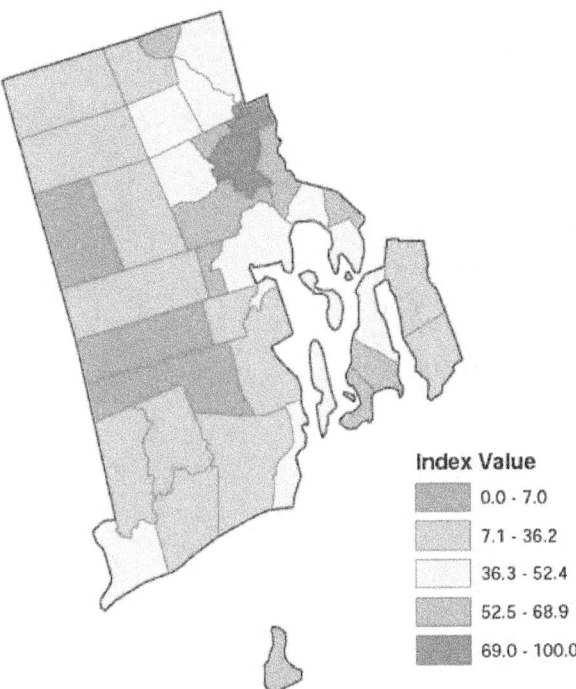

Index Value

- 0.0 - 7.0
- 7.1 - 36.2
- 36.3 - 52.4
- 52.5 - 68.9
- 69.0 - 100.0

Figure RI-11.—Planting priority index for county subdivisions. The higher the index value, the greater priority for planting.

Priority Areas for Tree Planting

Priority areas for planting tend to be highest in more urbanized areas due to higher population density (Fig. RI-11; Tables RI-15 through 17). These index values can also be produced using high resolution cover data to determine local planting priority areas (e.g., neighborhoods).

Urban Tree Benefits

The following forest attributes are estimated for the urban or community land in Rhode Island (Table RI-1). These are rough estimates of values. More localized data are needed for more precise estimates, but these values reveal first-order approximations.

- 17.5 million trees
- 3.3 million metric tons of C stored ($75.2 million value)
- 110,000 metric tons/year of C sequestered ($2.5 million value)
- 2,660 metric tons/year total pollution removal ($21.6 million value)
  - 44 metric tons/year of CO removed ($61,900 value)
  - 351 metric tons/year NO_2 removed ($3.5 million value)
  - 1,198 metric tons/year of O_3 removed ($11.9 million value)
  - 210 metric tons/year of SO_2 removed ($509,500 value)
  - 857 metric tons/year of PM_{10} removed ($5.7 million value)

Summary

The data presented in this report provide a better understanding of Rhode Island's urban and community forests. This information can be used to advance urban and community forestry policy and management that could improve environmental quality and human health throughout the state.

These data establish a baseline to assess future change and can be used to understand:

- Extent of the urban and community forest resource
- Variations in the resource across the state
- Magnitude and value of the urban and community forest resource
- Urban growth in Rhode Island
- Implications of policy decisions related to urban sprawl and urban and community forest management

ERMONT'S URBAN AND COMMUNITY FORESTS

Summary

Urban or community land in Vermont comprises about 2.9 percent of the state land area in 2000, a slight decrease from 1990. Statewide tree canopy cover averages 67.4 percent and tree cover in urban or community areas is about 36.4 percent, with 13.4 percent impervious surface cover and 42 percent of the total green space covered by tree canopy cover. Statewide, urban or community land in Vermont has an estimated 11.9 million trees, which store about 2.3 million metric tons of carbon ($52.4 million), and annually remove about 75,000 metric tons of carbon ($1.7 million) and 1,610 metric tons of air pollution ($14.2 million) (Table VT-1).

Tables VT-2 through VT-17 are not printed in this report but are available on the CD located on the inside back cover, and at http://www.nrs.fs.fed.us/data/urban.

Table VT-1.—Statewide summary of population, area, population density, tree canopy and impervious surface land cover, and urban tree benefits in urban, community, and urban or community areas.

ermont		Statewide	Urban [a]	Community [b]	Urban or community [c]
Population	2000	608,827	232,448	212,816	n/a
	1990	562,758	181,149	207,973	n/a
	% Change (1990-2000)	8.2	28.3	2.3	n/a
	% Total population (2000)	100.0	38.2	35.0	n/a
Total area	km^2 (2000)	24,900.8	382.7	592.0	745.0
	km^2 (1990)	24,900.8	396.0	594.5	759.4
	% Change (1990-2000)	0.0	-3.4	-0.4	-1.9
Land area	km^2 (2000)	23,939.2	376.8	534.3	684.9
	% Land area (2000)	100.0	1.6	2.2	2.9
	km^2 (1990)	23,939.2	391.1	536.9	699.8
	% Land area (1990)	100.0	1.6	2.2	2.9
	% Change (1990-2000)	0.0	-3.7	-0.5	-2.1
Population density (people/land area km^2)	2000	25.4	616.8	398.3	n/a
	1990	23.5	463.1	387.3	n/a
	% Change (1990-2000)	8.2	33.2	2.8	n/a
Tree canopy cover (2000)	km^2	16,141.1	115.9	200.2	249.0
	% Land area	67.4	30.8	37.5	36.4
	Per capita (m^2/person)	26,511.8	498.5	940.7	n/a
	% Canopy green space [d]	68.2	38.1	43.4	42.0
Total green space (2000) [e]	km^2	23,661.1	303.8	461.4	592.9
	% Land area	98.8	80.6	86.4	86.6
Available green space (2000) [f]	km^2	7,520.4	188.0	261.3	343.9
	% Land area	31.4	49.9	48.9	50.2
Impervious surface cover (2000)	km^2	278.1	73.0	72.9	92.0
	% Land area	1.2	19.4	13.6	13.4
	Per capita (m^2/person)	456.8	314.2	342.6	n/a
	Estimated number of trees	n/a	5,500,000	9,500,000	11,900,000
	Carbon				
	Carbon stored (metric tons)	n/a	1,100,000	1,800,000	2,300,000
	Carbon stored ($)	n/a	$25,100,000	$41,000,000	$52,400,000
	Carbon sequestered (metric tons/year)	n/a	35,000	60,000	75,000
	Carbon sequestered ($/year)	n/a	$798,000	$1,368,000	$1,710,000
	Pollution				
Urban tree benefits (2000)	CO removed (metric tons/year)	n/a	6	10	12
	CO removed ($/year)	n/a	$7,800	$13,500	$16,800
	NO_2 removed (metric tons/year)	n/a	76	132	164
	NO_2 removed ($/year)	n/a	$756,000	$1,306,000	$1,624,700
	O_3 removed (metric tons/year)	n/a	458	792	985
	O3 removed ($/year)	n/a	$4,541,000	$7,845,000	$9,758,000
	SO_2 removed (metric tons/year)	n/a	19	32	40
	SO_2 removed ($/year)	n/a	$45,400	$78,400	$97,500
	PM_{10} removed (metric tons/year)	n/a	191	330	411
	PM_{10} removed ($/year)	n/a	$1,264,900	$2,185,200	$2,718,300
	Total pollution removal (metric tons/year)	n/a	750	1,300	1,610
	Total pollution removal ($/year)	n/a	$6,600,000	$11,400,000	$14,200,000

[a] Urban land is based on population density and was delimited using the U.S. Census definitions of urbanized areas and urban clusters. [b] Community land is based on jurisdictional or political boundaries of communities based on U.S. Census definitions of incorporated or census designated places. [c] Urban or communities is land that is urban, community, or both. Communities may include all, some, or no urban land within their boundaries. [d] Canopy green space is the tree canopy cover divided by total green space. [e] Total green space is total area minus impervious surface cover minus water. [f] Available green space is total green space minus tree canopy cover (if the calculated value is less than 0, then value set at 0).

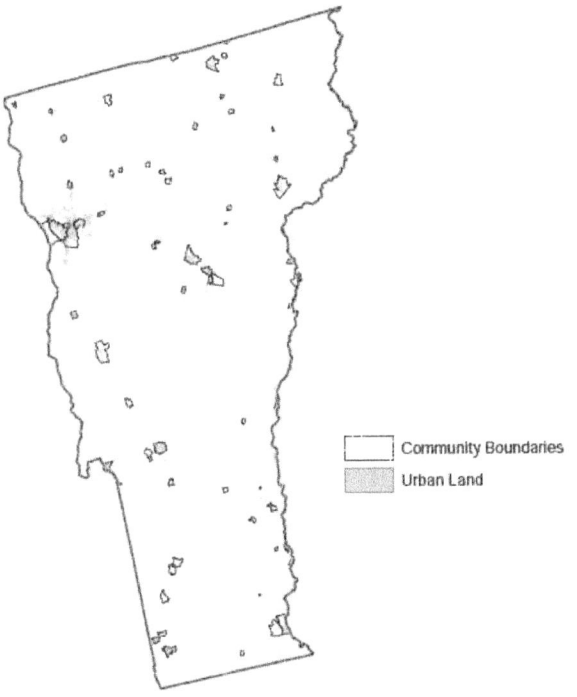

Community Boundaries
Urban Land

Figure VT-1.—Urban or community land in 2000;
urban area relative to community boundaries.

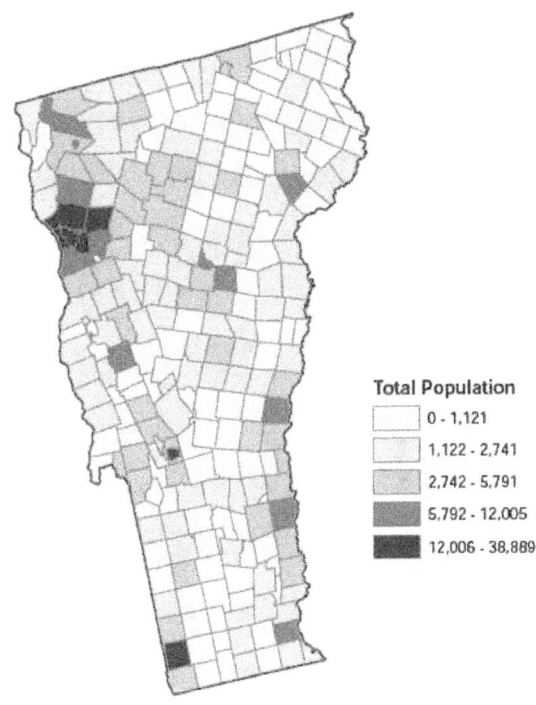

Total Population
0 - 1,121
1,122 - 2,741
2,742 - 5,791
5,792 - 12,005
12,006 - 38,889

Figure VT-2.—2000 Population within county
subdivision boundaries.

Human Population Characteristics and Trends

The population in Vermont increased 8.2 percent, from 562,758 in 1990
to 608,827 in 2000 (Table VT-1). In Vermont, 38.2 percent of the state's
population is in urban areas (Fig. VT-1), and 35 percent of the population is
within communities (Fig. VT-2).

Urban and Community Land

Urban land comprises 1.6 percent of the land area of Vermont, while lands
within communities make up 2.2 percent of the state (Fig. VT-1). Between
1990 and 2000, urban area and community land decreased slightly (Table
VT-1). Urban area in Vermont is projected to increase to 5.3 percent by
2050, based on average urban growth pattern of the 1990s (Nowak and
Walton 2005). Both urban land (attaining minimum population density)
and community land (political boundaries) decreased from 1990 to 2000.
The percentages are calculated using the total (water and land) area of the
geopolitical units derived from U.S. Census cartographic boundary data.
Percent urban land varied across the state (Fig. VT-3; Tables VT-2 through 4).

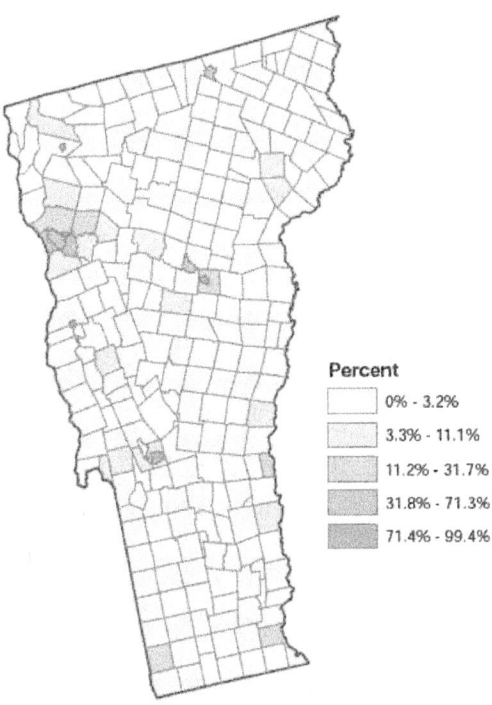

Percent
0% - 3.2%
3.3% - 11.1%
11.2% - 31.7%
31.8% - 71.3%
71.4% - 99.4%

Figure VT-3.—Percent of community
subdivision area classified as urban land
in 2000.

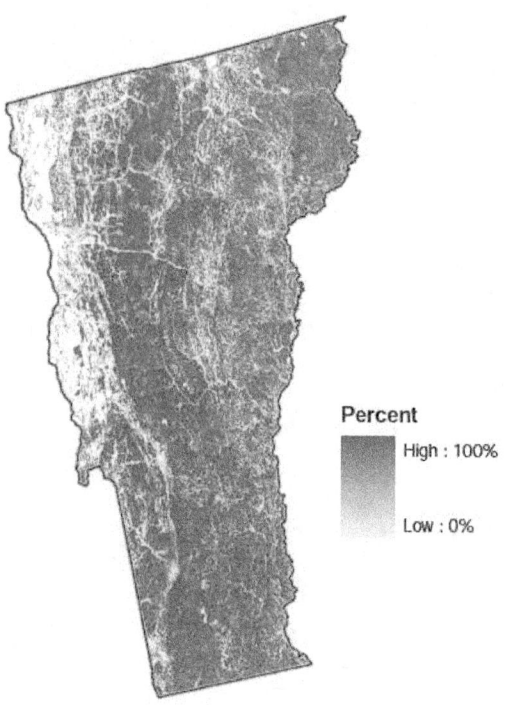

Figure VT-4.—Percentage tree canopy cover.

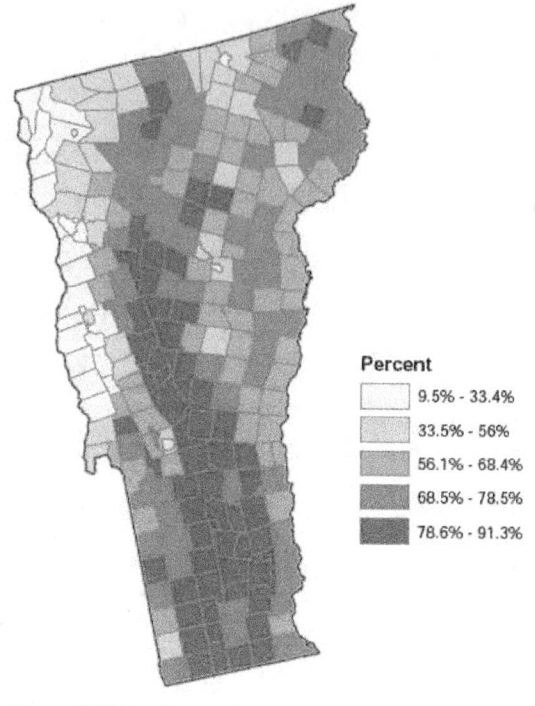

Percent
	9.5% - 33.4%
	33.5% - 56%
	56.1% - 68.4%
	68.5% - 78.5%
	78.6% - 91.3%

Figure VT-5.—Percentage tree canopy cover within county subdivisions.

Tree Canopy Cover Characteristics

Tree canopy cover in Vermont averages 67.4 percent (Fig. VT-4), with 98.8 percent total green space, 68.2 percent canopy green space, and 26,511.8 m^2 of canopy cover per capita. Average tree cover in urban areas in Vermont was 30.8 percent, with 80.6 percent total green space, 38.1 percent canopy green space, and 498.5 m^2 of canopy cover per capita. Within community lands in Vermont, average tree cover was 37.5 percent, with 86.4 percent total green space, 43.4 percent canopy green space, and 940.7 m^2 of canopy cover per capita (Table VT-1). Tree canopy cover, canopy green space, and tree cover per capita varied among communities, county subdivisions, and counties (Fig. VT-5 through 6; Tables VT-5 through 7).

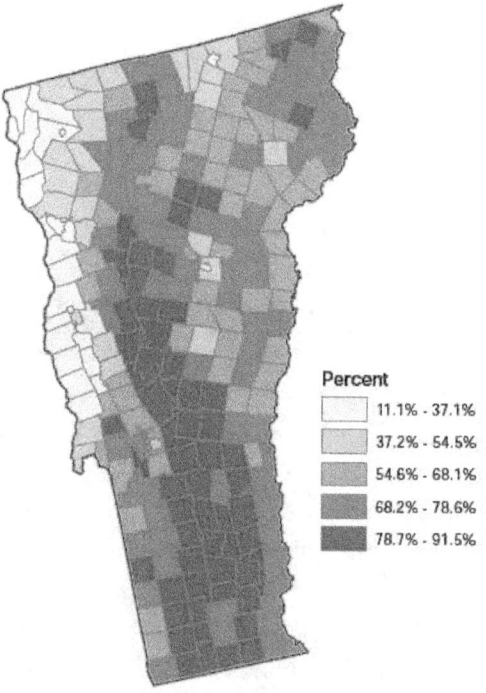

Percent
	11.1% - 37.1%
	37.2% - 54.5%
	54.6% - 68.1%
	68.2% - 78.6%
	78.7% - 91.5%

Figure VT-6.—Percentage tree canopy green space in county subdivisions.

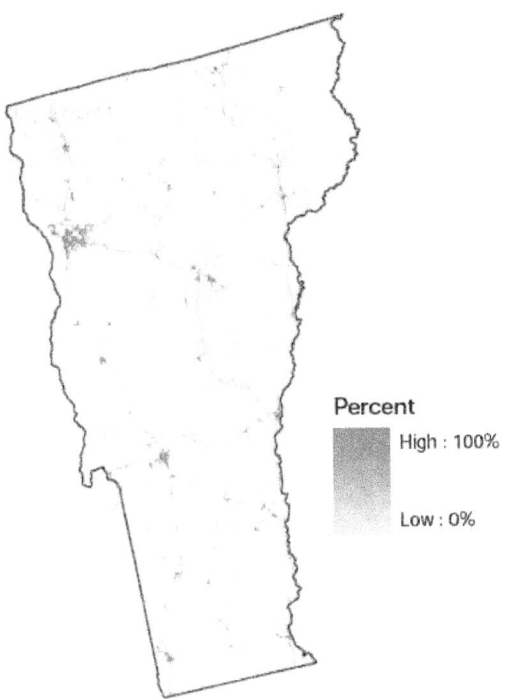

Figure VT-7.—Percentage impervious
surface cover.

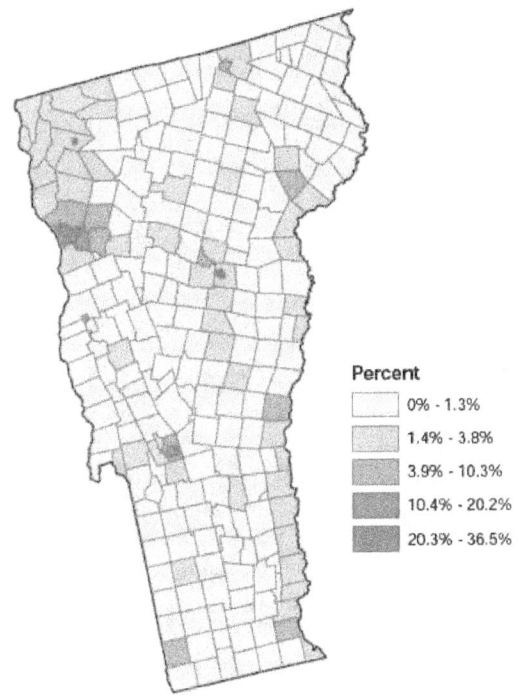

Percent
- 0% - 1.3%
- 1.4% - 3.8%
- 3.9% - 10.3%
- 10.4% - 20.2%
- 20.3% - 36.5%

Figure VT-8.—Percentage impervious
surface cover within county subdivisions.

Impervious Surface Cover Characteristics

Average impervious surface cover in Vermont is 1.2 percent of the land area (Fig. VT-7), with 456.8 m^2 of impervious surface cover per capita. Average impervious surface cover in urban areas was 19.4 percent, with 314.2 m^2 of impervious surface cover per capita. Within community lands in Vermont, average impervious surface cover was 13.6 percent with 342.6 m^2 of impervious surface cover per capita (Table VT-1). Impervious surface cover varied across the state (Fig. VT-8; Tables VT-5 through 7).

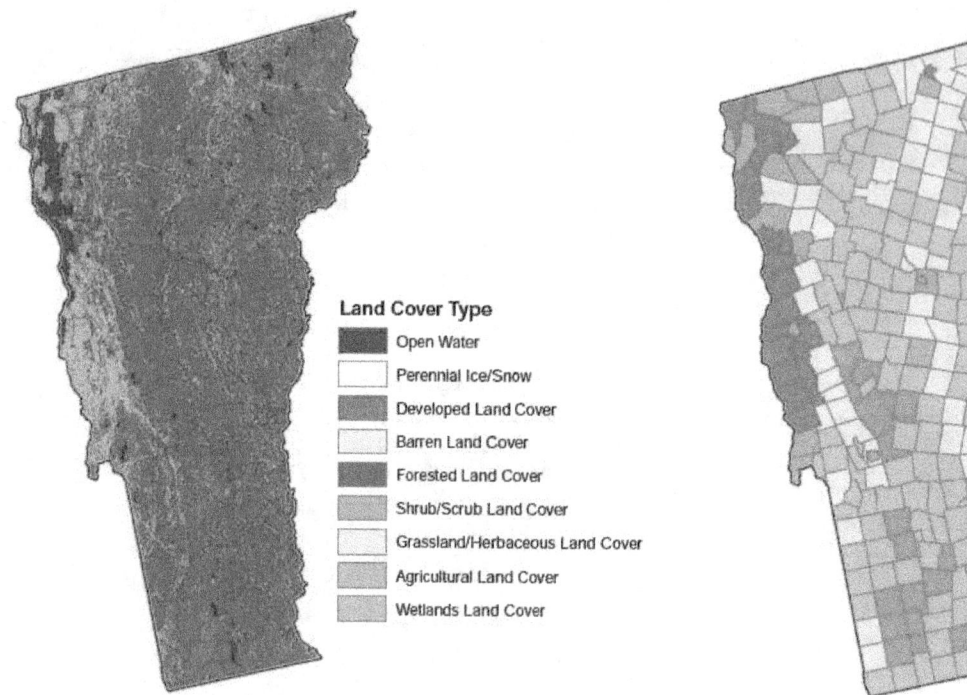

Land Cover Type

◼ Open Water
☐ Perennial Ice/Snow
▦ Developed Land Cover
☐ Barren Land Cover
◼ Forested Land Cover
▨ Shrub/Scrub Land Cover
☐ Grassland/Herbaceous Land Cover
▨ Agricultural Land Cover
▨ Wetlands Land Cover

Figure VT-9.—Classified land cover.

Rating

▨ Excellent
▨ Very Good
☐ Good
▨ Fair
◼ Poor

Figure VT-10.—Relative comparisons of urban and community forests for county subdivisions.

Classified Land-cover Characteristics

Vermont's landcover is dominated by forest land (Fig. VT-9). The characteristics as a percent of the total land area in Vermont are (Tables VT-8 through 10):

- Forested—74.5 percent
- Agricultural—17.8 percent
- Developed—5.5 percent
- Scrub/Shrub—1.5 percent
- Wetland—0.3 percent
- Grassland—0.3 percent
- Barren—0.1 percent

Relative Comparisons of Urban and Community Forests

Out of the 67 Vermont communities, none received a rating of excellent and 22 received a rating of poor (Table VT-12). Of the 255 county subdivisions, 19 had a rating of excellent and 23 were rated poor (Fig. VT-10, Table VT-13); and out of 14 counties, two were given a rating of excellent and three were given a rating of poor (Table VT -14). Variability of assessment scores is a product of the difference in land cover distributions and the percentage of canopy cover within the population density classes and mapping zones (Fig. VT-10; Tables VT-11 through 14).

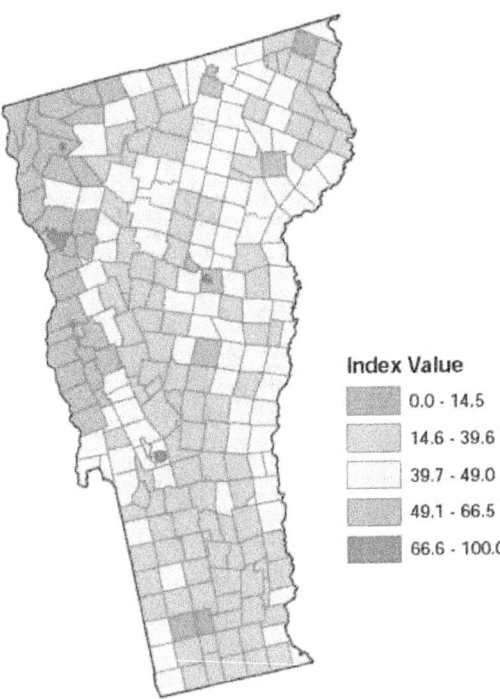

Index Value

	0.0 - 14.5
	14.6 - 39.6
	39.7 - 49.0
	49.1 - 66.5
	66.6 - 100.0

Figure VT-11.—Planting priority index for county subdivisions. The higher the index value, the greater priority for planting.

Priority Areas for Tree Planting

Priority areas for planting tend to be highest in more urbanized areas due to higher population density (Fig. VT-11; Tables VT-15 through 17). These index values can also be produced using high resolution cover data to determine local planting priority areas (e.g. neighborhoods).

Urban Tree Benefits

The following forest attributes are estimated for the urban or community land in Vermont (Table VT-1). These are rough estimates of values. More localized data are needed for more precise estimates, but these values reveal first-order approximations.

- 11.9 million trees
- 2.3 million metric tons of C stored ($52.4 million value)
- 75,000 metric tons/year of C sequestered ($1.7 million value)
- 1,610 metric tons/year total pollution removal ($14.2 million value)
  - 12 metric tons/year of CO removed ($16,800 value)
  - 164 metric tons/year NO_2 removed ($1.6 million value)
  - 985 metric tons/year of O_3 removed ($9.8 million value)
  - 40 metric tons/year of SO_2 removed ($97,500 value)
  - 411 metric tons/year of PM_{10} removed ($2.7 million value)

Summary

The data presented in this report provide a better understanding of Vermont's urban and community forests. This information can be used to advance urban and community forestry policy and management that could improve environmental quality and human health throughout the state.

These data establish a baseline to assess future change and can be used to understand:

- Extent of the urban and community forest resource
- Variations in the resource across the state
- Magnitude and value of the urban and community forest resource
- Urban growth in Vermont
- Implications of policy decisions related to urban sprawl and urban and community forest management

Dwyer, J.F.; Nowak, D.J.; Noble, H.M.; Sisinni, S.M. 2000. **Assessing our nation's urban forests: connecting people with ecosystems in the 21st century.** Gen. Tech. Rep. PNW-490. Portland, OR: U.S. Department of Agriculture, Forest Service, Pacific Northwest Research Station. 540 p.

Fankhauser, S. 1994. **The social costs of greenhouse gas emissions: an expected value approach.** The Energy Journal. 15(2): 157-184.

Homer, C.; Huang, C.; Yang, L.; Wylie, B.; Coan, M. 2004. **Development of a 2001 national land cover database for the United States.** Photogrammetric Engineering and Remote Sensing. 70(7): 829-840.

Homer, C.G.; Gallant, A. 2001. **Partitioning the conterminous United States into mapping zones for Landsat TM land cover mapping.** Unpublished U.S. Geologic Survey report. http://landcover.usgs.gov/pdf/homer.pdf. (1 August 2008).

Homer, C.; Dewitz. J.; Fry, J.; Coan, M.; Hossain, N.; Larson, C.; Herold, N.; McKerrow, A.; VanDriel, J.N.; Wickham, J. 2007. **Completion of the 2001 national land cover database for the coterminous United States.** Photogrammetric Engineering and Remote Sensing. 73(4): 337-341.

Murray, F.J.; Marsh,L.; Bradford, P.A. 1994. **New York state energy plan Vol. II: issue reports.** Albany, NY: New York State Energy Research and Development Authority.

National Climatic Data Center. 2000. **Integrated surface hourly observations 2000.** Silver Spring, MD: U.S. Department of Commerce, National Oceanic and Atmospheric Administration. [CD-ROM].

Nowak, D.J. 1993. **Compensatory value of an urban forest: an application of tree-value formula.** Journal of Arboriculture. 19(3): 173-177.

Nowak, D.J. 1994a. **Atmospheric carbon dioxide reduction by Chicago's urban forest.** In: McPherson, E.G; Nowak, D.J.; Rowntree, R.A. Chicago's urban forest ecosystem: results of the Chicago urban forest climate project. Gen. Tech. Rep. NE-186. Radnor, PA: U.S. Department of Agriculture, Forest Service, Northeastern Research Station: 83-94.

Nowak, D.J. 1994b. **Urban forest structure: the state of Chicago's urban forest.** In: McPherson, E.G; Nowak, D.J.; Rowntree, R.A. Chicago's urban forest ecosystem: results of the Chicago urban forest climate project. Gen. Tech. Rep. NE-186. Radnor, PA: U.S. Department of Agriculture, Forest Service Northeastern Research Station: 3-18 and 140-164 [appendix].

Nowak, D.J.; Crane, D.E. 2000. **The Urban Forest Effects (UFORE) model: quantifying urban forest structure and functions.** In: Hansen, M.; Burk, T., eds. Integrated tools for natural resources inventories in the 21st century, proceedings of the IUFRO conference; 1998 August 16-20; Boise, ID. Gen. Tech. Rep. NC-212. St. Paul, MN: U.S. Department of Agriculture, Forest Service, North Central Research Station: 714-720.

Nowak, D.J.; Crane, D.E.. 2002. **Carbon storage and sequestration by urban trees in the United States.** Environmental Pollution. 116(3): 381-389.

Nowak, D.J.; Crane, D.E.; Stevens, J.C. 2001a. **Syracuse's urban forest resource.** In: Nowak, D.J.; O'Connor, P., comps. Syracuse urban forest master plan: guiding the city's forest resource in the 21st century. Gen. Tech. Rep. NE-287. Newtown Square, PA: U.S. Department of Agriculture, Forest Service, Northeastern Research Station: 9-14.

Nowak, D.J.; Crane, D.E.; Stevens, J.C. 2006d. **Air pollution removal by urban trees and shrubs in the United States.** Urban Forestry and Urban Greening. 4: 115-123.

Nowak, D.J.; Hoehn, R.; Crane, D.E.; Stevens, J.C.; Walton, J.T. 2006a. **Assessing urban forest effects and values: Casper, WY's urban forest.** Res. Bull. NRS-4. Newtown Square, PA: U.S. Department of Agriculture, Forest Service, Northeastern Research Station. 20 p.

Nowak, D.J.; Hoehn, R.; Crane, D.E.; Stevens, J.C.; Walton, J.T. 2006b. **Assessing urban forest effects and values: Minneapolis' urban forest.** Res. Bull. NE-166. Newtown Square, PA: U.S. Department of Agriculture, Forest Service, Northeastern Research Station. 20 p.

Nowak, D.J.; Hoehn, R.; Crane, D.E.; Stevens, J.C.; Walton, J.T. 2006c. **Assessing urban forest effects and values: Washington D.C.'s urban forest.** Resour. Bull. NRS-1. Newtown Square, PA: U.S. Department of Agriculture, Forest Service, Northeastern Research Station. 24 p.

Nowak, D.J.; Hoehn, R.; Crane, D.E.; Stevens, J.C.; Walton, J.T. 2007a. **Assessing urban forest effects and values: New York's urban forest.** Resour. Bull. NRS-9. Newtown Square, PA: U.S. Department of Agriculture, Forest Service, Northeastern Research Station. 22 p.

Nowak, D.J.; Hoehn, R.; Crane, D.E.; Stevens, J.C.; Walton, J.T. 2007b. **Assessing urban forest effects and values: Philadelphia's urban forest.** Resour. Bull. NRS-7. Newtown Square, PA: U.S. Department of Agriculture, Forest Service, Northeastern Research Station. 22 p.

Nowak, D.J.; Hoehn, R.; Crane, D.E.; Stevens, J.C.; Walton, J.T. 2007c. **Assessing urban forest effects and values: San Francisco's urban forest.** Resour. Bull. NRS-8.

Newtown Square, PA: U.S. Department of Agriculture, Forest Service, Northeastern Research Station. 22 p.

Nowak, D.J.; Noble, M.H.; Sisinni, S.M.; Dwyer J.F. 2001b. **People and trees: assessing the U.S. urban forest resource.** Journal of Forestry. 99(3): 37-42.

Nowak, D.J.; Walton, J.T.; Dwyer, J.F.; Kaya, L.G.; Myeong, S. 2005. **The increasing influence of urban environments on U.S. forest management.** Journal of Forestry. 103(8): 377-382.

Nowak, D.J.; Walton, J.T. 2005. **Projected urban growth and its estimated impact on the U.S. forest resource (2000-2050).** Journal of Forestry. 103(8): 383-389.

Ottinger, R.L.; Wooley D.R.; Robinson N.A.; Hodas D.R.; Babb S.E.; Buchanan S.C.; Chernick P.L.; Caverhill E; Krupnick A.; Fritsche U. 1990. **Environmental costs of electricity.** White Plains, NY: Oceana Publications. 769 p.

U.S. Census Bureau. n.d. **www.census.gov**. (January 2007).

U.S. Department of Labor Bureau of Labor Statistics. n.d. **www.bls.gov/ppi/** (June 2007).

U.S. Environmental Protection Agency. 2003. **National air quality and emissions trends report: 2003 special studies edition.** Research Triangle Park, NC: U.S. Environmental Protection Agency, Office of Air Quality Planning and Standards, Emissions Monitoring and Analysis Division.

U.S. Environmental Protection Agency. n.d. **www.epa.gov/oar/data** (June 2008).

U.S. Department of Interior, Geologic Survey. 2008. **Multi-resolution land characteristics consortium.** www.mrlc.gov. (1 August 2008).

Walton, J.T. 2005. **An investigation of national tree canopy assessments applied to urban forestry.** Syracuse, NY: State University of New York, College of Environmental Science and Forestry. 95 p. Ph.D. dissertation.

Yang, L.; Huang, C.; Homer, C.G.; Wylie, B.K.; Coan, M.J. 2003. **An approach for mapping large-area impervious surfaces: synergistic use of Landsat-7 ETM+ and high spatial resolution imagery.** Canadian Journal of Remote Sensing. 29(2): 230–240.

Zhu, Z. 1994. **Forest density mapping in the lower 48 states: a regression procedure.** Res. Pap. SO-280. New Orleans, LA: U.S. Department of Agriculture, Forest Service, Southern Research Station. 11 p.

The following tables are generated to support state reports on urban and community forests of the New England States of Connecticut, Maine, Massachusetts, New Hampshire, Rhode Island, and Vermont. For specific state data tables use the CD accompanying this publication and search within the regional or state folder, or go to: http://www.nrs.fs.fed.us/data/urban.

Region Specific Table:

Table B.—NLCD versus photo-interpreted values for mapping zones

State Specific Tables:

Table 1.—Statewide summary of population, area, population density, tree canopy and impervious surface land cover, and urban tree benefits in urban, community, and urban or community areas.

Table 2.—2000 population characteristics, population change (1990-2000), and percent of land classified as urban within communities.

Table 3.—2000 population characteristics, population change (1990-2000), percent of land classified as urban or as communities within county subdivisions.

Table 4.—2000 population characteristics, population change (1990-2000), percent of land classified as urban or as communities within counties.

Table 5.—Tree canopy and impervious surface cover characteristics by community.

Table 6.—Tree canopy and impervious surface cover characteristics by county subdivision.

Table 7.—Tree canopy and impervious surface cover characteristics by county.

Table 8.—Land area, tree canopy cover, and available green space distributed within generalized land cover categories for communities.

Table 9.—Land area, tree canopy cover, and available green space distributed within generalized land cover categories for county subdivisions.

Table 10.—Land area, tree canopy cover, and available green space distributed within generalized land cover categories for counties.

Table 11.—Statistical summary of mapping zone values used to calculate urban and community forestry assessment.

Table 12.—Urban and community forestry assessment by community.

Table 13.—Urban and community forestry assessment by county subdivisions.

Table 14.—Urban and community forestry assessment by counties.

Table 15.—Planting priority index for communities.

Table 16.—Planting priority index for county subdivisions.

Table 17.—Planting priority index for counties.